How to Make It Through the Day

How to Make It Through the Day

John Carmody

THE UPPER ROOM
Nashville, Tennessee

How to Make It Through the Day

Scripture quotations not otherwise identified are from the Revised Standard
Version of the Bible, copyrighted 1946, 1952, and © 1971 by the Division of
Christian Education, National Council of the Churches of Christ in the
United States of America, and are used by permission.

Scripture passages designated KJV are from the King James Version of the
Bible.

Book and cover design: Harriette Bateman

First Printing: February 1985 (7)
Library of Congress Catalog Card Number: 84-051826
ISBN 0-8358-0491-7
Printed in the United States of America

IN MEMORY OF
Larry Waurin

Contents

Preface

This book falls in the category of Christian self-help. On the one hand, it depends on Christian faith and assumes that God's grace is the final cause of all our best achievements. On the other hand, it believes that we can do a great deal to help ourselves, since God has given us good minds and decent hearts. Reflecting on the interaction between these two aspects of the Christian message, as I have seen them work out in pastoral practice, I have been led to conceive a regime by which many people might improve the quality of their lives and increase their stores of joy and peace. In the background of this regime lie the theoretical works of Bernard Lonergan, whose studies of human understanding and theological method lay out a rich interpretation of the person's progress to wisdom and courage. In the foreground lie the people I've been privileged to work with in situations of pastoral counseling.

My thanks to my wife, Denise, for critical suggestions; to Karla Kraft, for cheerful and expert typing; and to Larry Waurin, one of the people I first counseled, who tragically died of AIDS (acquired immune deficiency syndrome) in 1983 and haunted my writing of this book with bittersweet memories.

Introduction:
California Suffering

Barbara

Years ago, when I was in California, I met a very unhappy woman. She was attractive, in her early thirties, had two handsome young children, and was in the middle of a messy divorce. I tried to give her some company, the sympathetic ear of a fellow-Christian also struggling. Over the course of six months or so we had several serious conversations. The main thing I learned, and have pondered ever since, is how difficult many people find it to gain peace of mind.

Barbara had been in love with her husband since high school. While he had gone off to college she had trained as a nurse. They married when he graduated, and she worked while he did further studies. Then he got a good job and they started a family. Things began to come apart shortly after they moved to California. His job involved a lot of traveling and socializing. Soon he was away more than he was home, and Barbara found signs that he was seeing other women. They fought, reconciled, spoke with their pastor, and promised they would make a new start. He would drop the other women and do better by her and the kids. She would try to understand the pressures of his job. But it didn't work. In a few months he was back to his old ways, and she was again miserable. This pattern of fighting, reconciling, and fighting again went on for a couple of years, until finally he told her he had become serious about another woman and wanted a divorce. I met Barbara about a year after that, when her ten years of marriage were about to go down the drain, and her faith was being severely tested.

Barbara talked to me because I was a priest assigned to her church while I did graduate studies at a nearby university. The first thing that impressed me was her struggle to be honest, the second thing was her poor self-image. When she began to open up she would say things like: "Look at what a mess I am. I used to be pretty and happy. Now I can't stand to look at myself in the mirror. I can't stand to think of what a failure I must be in God's eyes. I don't really know why all this has happened. Jack says I'm stupid and have no imagination. Part of me says he must be right. I'm sure I could have been more understanding. But another part of me knows he's wrong and that he really hasn't been fair. I was so hurt when I learned about the other woman. But the worst thing was his treatment of the boys. The last two years he barely gave them the time of day."

For a while I just tried to listen sympathetically. I hadn't had much pastoral experience, and Barbara was very attractive. The last thing she needed was more emotional complication, so I tried to be very careful. After a while, however, I became convinced that I had to be more direct. She kept going over and over the same things, putting herself further and further down. So one day I said: "Look. Let's try to get a few basic things clear. First, your former husband, whatever his brains and other virtues, has hardly been a model of Christian fidelity. In any objective view, at least 80 percent of the blame belongs to him. Second, you are beautiful and you are competent. Your life is far from over. I see how you treat your kids. You're wonderfully warm and loving. I wish you'd treat yourself half as well. Let's stop poring over all your weaknesses, stop assuming that God can't bring good out of this, and start building on your strengths.''

So we did. Slowly, bit by bit, we worked out a way for Barbara to start moving ahead. There were many more painful times. Her scars took a long time to fade. But gradually she became able to look the past in the eye, examine her conscience peacefully, face herself in the mirror, and not be paralyzed. Eventually she moved back East, got a job as a factory nurse, and after a few years remarried. Her mother helped, some friends pitched in, but she did most of it by herself. My part, as I reflect on it now, was very minor. I just happened to be the person who was available when she needed to switch onto a new track. She may think of me now and then, and if she does she's probably grateful. But actually, she did more for me than I did for her, because she was the one who forced me to bring all my training down from the clouds and put it to work practically. She was the one who made me lay out a clear Christian path to peace of mind.

This book is just an elaboration of the method I started working on with Barbara. It's really quite simple and has no gimmicks of which I'm aware. It doesn't say I'm OK, you're OK, and together we're great. It doesn't say the Lord will wipe away every tear and give you a pink Cadillac. It simply says that you *can* bear looking at yourself, *can* face your pains, *can* find strengths to build upon, because the God who made you has done good work. It says that because you have a mind and are able to think, you, like Barbara, can get a handle on your problems.

To be sure, Barbara had a lot going for her. She was pretty and she had a profession. But she also had a lot going against her. She was no brighter than average, her faith was not very reflective, and the man she had loved with all her heart had kicked her in the teeth. It was only when she became able to think clearly about her situation that her life started to improve. It was only when she could face herself and her God that her self started to heal. With a little help, you can start to think clearly about your situation. If you want, your self can start to heal. There is no magic in my method. All it uses is your capacity to stop, think, and respond to the Spirit's leadings.

Paul

About the time I was dealing with Barbara an equally unhappy man came along. With him I had much less success, so most of what he taught me was negative: things not to do. Paul was an expert in computers, lured to California's "silicon valley" in the late sixties, when big things started to happen there. I met him because he called my church, obviously very drunk, and asked for someone to rescue him from his bar. I found him propped on a stool, stupid and bleary-eyed. I took him to his apartment, left my name and address, and suggested that when he sobered up he give me a call. He did and I started seeing him regularly.

Paul had money, brains, and bad memories of home and school. He was in his midthirties, single, and had very few friends. Apparently he was good at his job but clumsy about almost everything else. He had been brought up in a rather devout family, but most of his faith had slipped away during graduate studies in chemistry. When I tried to get him to face his most obvious problem, the heavy drinking, he would veer off into abstract questions about faith and science. Foolishly, I let him veer, although I knew from experience with alcoholics in my own family that such talk is almost worthless. A traveling preacher that Paul met saw things much more clearly. The preacher was on the road peddling Gideon Bibles and ended up next to Paul on a train. Paul insisted that he meet with me, to discuss what sort of religion Paul might be able to accept. The preacher looked me over, cocked an eye at Paul, and said: "Son, I don't know how you size up old Paul here, but for my money his problem ain't with religion. Old Paul's a drunk, plain and simple, and he won't know no peace till he admits it."

Well, Paul wouldn't admit it, wouldn't even face the possibility. I never got him to see the pattern of his weekend binges or to take stock of his shaking hand and bleary eye. So I indulged his desire to argue about religion and tried to find useful things for him to do in his spare time. I introduced him to people that might befriend him, gave him good books on theology and prayer, and suggested such helps as Alcoholics Anonymous, psychotherapy, and programs of physical fitness. All to no avail. Eventually Paul drifted away, sensing I'd run out of ideas. I'm afraid I left him little better for having met me.

If today I compare Barbara and Paul, what stands out is the difference in their abilities to come to terms with themselves. Paul was brighter, better educated, and much more deeply disturbed. His problems were rooted deep in his genes or family history, way below anything I could touch. He would roll himself in a

ball like a porcupine, guarding every flank with prick-
ly quills. That was absurd, of course, because most
nights he could barely stand up. But his resistance to
the Spirit's call for reform was stronger than his
misery. He needed help a lot more specialized than
anything I could provide.

Barbara, on the other hand, was basically healthy.
Her problems largely came from the outside. She was
stunned and hurt, because the person to whom she
had opened herself most intimately had betrayed her
badly. Basically, though, all she needed was time to
heal, quiet her depths, pray honestly, and gain a better
perspective. Once she stopped running in circles and
came to grips with her situation, her life began to
move ahead again. From my vantage point, the one
thing Barbara was able to do, and Paul wasn't, was to
begin in the present and take first things first. Where
Paul just would not deal with his drinking, Barbara
would deal with her hurt and anger. Where I could
not get Paul to pay attention to the obvious first
question, Barbara was able to take a deep breath, stir
up her faith, and plunge in.

Some of this difference, of course, may have
been due to sexual conditioning. Perhaps Barbara had
been socialized to great docility, Paul to more indepen-
dence and resistance. Or maybe I was kinder to
Barbara, less skillful with Paul. Whatever, Barbara
soon was able to name her feelings, face her fears,
and look hard at the inside of things. Paul lived on the
outside of himself, out of touch with his deepest
feelings. If my general experience is valid, most men
don't catch up religiously with women until they're
fifty or so, when slowing down physically finally
makes them at least a little bit reflective. This is
tragic, because without reflection there is no good

judgment, no wisdom, no appreciation of the Spirit's movements.

From these two character sketches let me draw several suggestions about how to use this book. First, the book depends on your willingness to try to stop, think, and pray. If you are a man younger than fifty, you may have to put forth some effort. If you are a woman, you should not find reflection especially hard.

Second, the book assumes a certain basic mental health and so is not suited to perhaps one-fourth of the people who are likely to pick it up. If you regularly drink too much, or have long been depressed, or are so violent you get into trouble with the law, you should take yourself, without any shame, to more specialized sources of help: Alcoholics Anonymous, a psychiatrist, a local counseling center. You would not expect a religious book like this to heal a broken arm. You shouldn't expect it to solve serious emotional problems. The other three-fourths of my likely readers, who simply feel down pretty often, frequently need to pull themselves back together and deepen their sense of God's love, should be able to use the method described here without any danger. In their case, the way to begin a process of healing is as simple as paying attention.

1.

Paying Attention

Here and Now

The only time that is fully real is the present. Yesterday is old news and tomorrow is full of maybes. This is obvious enough, when one reflects on it, but it takes most of us many years to realize its full implications. So most of us spend a great deal of our time daydreaming about the past or worrying about the future. Not realizing the value of the real bird we have in hand, we leave the present to go rooting in past or future bushes. As a result, the personal business that should stand highest on our agenda often never gets done. What is this personal business? Finding peace of mind, and so happiness, right here and now. Learning to live so that we savor each day, waste none of the precious moments God has given us.

As I began this line of thought, I decided to test my own performance. ("Physician, heal thyself.") Checking on what was nibbling at the edge of my mind, distracting me whenever I gave it the least chance, I found that I was worrying, trivially enough, about the rain lashing our new house and yard. Our lot pitches rather steeply, and we don't yet have strong ground cover. So any hard rain washes away quite a bit of earth, leaving deeper and deeper gullies. I'm not yet sure what to do about this or about the landscaping in general. The best I've been able to do is assure myself that as soon as the rains stop we'll attack the whole problem. Meanwhile, I feel uneasy about the erosion, and I let it worry me. Such a little thing, in any big picture, yet it eats away at my peace.

Almost always we can cut in half the things eating away at our peace by facing them directly, finding what they really amount to against the backdrop of God's mystery. Almost always our problems do most of their hurt indirectly, working in the dark. When we take them on straightforwardly and drag them out into the light, they usually shrink considerably.

Consider, for example, the fear many people have of losing their jobs. This fear has a solid basis. In hard times, very few jobs are completely protected. So when state budgets tilt toward a deficit, many state workers begin to worry about the future. When interest rates go sky-high, many builders turn green around the gills. To the dismay of millions, we have learned that our modern economy is very fragile. While all kinds of good works cry out to be done, and all kinds of people are desperate for a job, our economy often is unable to match them up. Consequently, many of our people sleep badly; they don't have the peace that is one of the Spirit's best gifts.

Now, getting one's mind into the present, learning to live here and now, obviously is not going to solve the country's economic problems. To face one's fears directly does not drive real problems away. What it can do, though, is get real problems out on the table, where we can go to work on them and force them to fit into God's overall scheme. What it can do is stop the losses of energy and spirit we suffer because we are anxious about vague unknowns. The beginning of good mental health or robust faith is a level gaze at one's actual situation. If one's actual situation is that one has a job and that no sure threats to this job have been announced, then one can say: "Right now it is useless to worry." Next week, when the new budget figures have been announced, it may be quite sensible to worry, or even to start planning one's next moves. All things can indeed change. But if, right now, no definite sword hangs over one's head, one is a fool to ruin the present with false worry. As the gospel of Christ says, "Sufficient unto the day is the evil thereof" (Matt. 6:34 KJV). Tomorrow can take care of itself.

So I say to myself: *Get your mind off the rain and the erosion. Put it back on your work. You know you can't do anything about this problem until the better weather comes. You've already set aside time and money to deal with it then. You're a dimwit if you let next month's project ruin your present peace and work. You preach common sense to the world and faith in a provident Creator. Why don't you show a little faith and common sense yourself?*

So I say to you, my readers: We start to come to grips with our problems, begin to get our thoughts and emotions under control, when we focus on the here and now. What's going on inside you here and now? What's really on your mind, really troubling your peace in the Spirit? Is it a lack of job security that's making you edgy? Are you depressed by the constant fall of rain? Or is it old business you're chewing over, sins or hurts from months ago? If you don't feel clear and all-together, if you feel clouded and divided, there must be a reason. Our moods are not accidents.

Of course, fatigue and illness do shape us. A change in diet or exercise might help. But more times than not we are depressed, cloudy rather than clear, because of guilt or fear or resentment we don't even recognize. Most of our unhappiness comes from little demons doing their work in the dark. When we stop, take stock, lay our consciences open to God, and follow our distressing feelings back to their sources, we shine a light on these little demons. Then, seeing them, giving them names, we can start to shoo their unwarranted influences away.

Seeing is not the whole solution. More hard work may remain. But seeing is the beginning, the necessary first step. When we own up to what's going on inside us here and how, we start the journey to peace of mind, accept the Spirit's invitation.

Regular Stopping

Recently I had dinner with friends who had relatives visiting. One of the relatives was about forty, the mother of four kids. When the talk turned to education, she became quite obnoxious, preaching to all of us about ,the values *her* kids were going to learn. They were going to grow up honest, helpful, and untouched by any of "this religious nonsense."

Moved by the charm of her speech, I asked just which nonsense she meant. "Oh, you know, those screaming fundamentalists and those sick introverts." Not the clearest of groupings, but nonetheless a start. Well, bracketing the fundamentalists, just what was it that bothered her about the introverts? "They keep trying to make something out of nothing. They're always scraping their insides. There's no mystery to life. You just get up in the morning and do what you have to do. I don't feel any need for introspection. I don't feel any need for God. I stay on the surface of things and do just fine.'' And so she did—except for the anger in her voice, the darting fear in her eyes, the jut of her jaw. She was daring me to disagree, almost hoping I'd make a fight.

What I wanted to do was hold up a full-length mirror, play back an accurate tape. If she could see her tension, hear her aggression, she might back off for a moment, stop the game, and let her real self speak. For, clearly, the woman was both bright and troubled. Clearly, she wanted the best for her kids and feared they would not get it. Having left the religious formation she herself had received, she didn't know what to put in its place. Half of her tried to jam herself into a busy practicality, all bustle and doing. The other half screamed that it didn't fit, was bending her all out of shape. If she was an advertisement for atheism, faith was in quite good condition.

The fact is, we are built, coded, primed for *both* action and reflection. The fact is, neither extroversion nor introversion alone allows us to be fully human. Whatever the emphasis of our personality, active or reflective, we need the other side as a balance or complement. Nature itself seems to recognize this, tending to make the first half of the life cycle more active, the second half more reflective. Indeed, most wise people develop a rhythm of action and reflection, an interchange between doing and analyzing.

If we seldom reflect, set what we've been doing in the overall context of the divine mystery, we tend to keep hitting our heads against the wall, making the same mistakes. If we seldom act, we rarely test our ideas or our courage, never put our faith on the line. Full maturity demands a cycle of doing our best, analyzing the results, and then trying to do better next time. Most immaturity comes from being either mindless or do-nothing. To grow as the best part of us wants, we have to learn to act and reflect and then act again.

How might this happen? By building in a regular stopping, an habitual time for religious reflection. Most of us have to *do* some things—work, care for kids, keep up a house or apartment. We can't avoid at least a minimal kind of activity. But we don't *have* to reflect regularly. We can go for days with little introspection or prayer. Probably we do reflect about some things each day. We think about the past, plan for the future, and send up little petitions to God. But probably we don't do this in a disciplined, formal, regular way. Probably we don't link our reflections to the here and now as profitably as we might. Therefore, let me try to sell you on the merits of regular religious reflection.

The great merit in stopping regularly to reflect is that it gives you a simple, reliable way to come to grips with all your everyday problems and make solid connections between them and Christ. If you know that each morning, before you head out to work, you are going to have fifteen, twenty, or thirty minutes to get yourself together, find out what's happening inside, and ask God to bless your day, you can be confident that you're not going to have too many unpleasant surprises. More often than not, you will have seen trouble starting to brew, realized something was getting on your nerves, long before it reached crisis proportions.

Of course, your regular stopping doesn't have to take place in the morning. You may prefer to do it at the end of the day, like giving your desk a final tidying, adding up your accounts one last time. The time and precise format are secondary. Of primary importance are (1) the regularity and (2) the here and now focus.

If you make a little patch of quiet a regular practice, it will grow on you. Even if you're quite extroverted and nervous, you'll soon come to find it settling, soothing. For just as you're made to stir up your energies, hit the bricks, and get things moving; so you're made to wind down, kick off your shoes, and let the battles be done. It feels good to return to one's center, to reorient oneself to God's whole. It heals wounds and reknits nerves. We're not made to work only on the surface. An important part of us lies deeper. When we start to feed this deeper part, nursing it with quiet, we feel better about ourselves, more whole and balanced. Then we're less likely to embarrass our family or ourselves by spilling out anger we didn't even know we had.

In Greece the temple of Apollo at Delphi is inscribed with the words: "Know thyself." The gateway to knowing ourselves is regular stopping for reflection, each day asking the Spirit to shed light.

Attending to the Inside

When the angry lady I met at my friends' home challenged me with her scorn for reflection, I wanted to hold up a mirror. Not having one, I had to listen to more of her preaching. So I learned that religion was not her only whipping boy. She was equally down on poetry, research, and athletics. From her standpoint as an insurance salesperson, they all were a waste of time. If she had her way, her kids' schooling would include none of them. School ought to prepare kids for the real world. In the real world, the business of life was business.

My friends had heard all of this, of course. Since she was their relative they had to take her in, and taking her in meant hearing her many opinions. I was a new audience, so I got most of her attention. I bore up pretty well for a while, making noncommital replies or trying to throw in a little humor. Finally, however, the woman got to me. *Arrogance,* I told myself, *I can take. Ignorance I can handle. Arrogant ignorance is too much. It's time to expose the lady's superficiality.* So I did, telling her that with such a mother her kids didn't need enemies, and that if she succeeded they'd be just like herself: stupid, superficial, and neurotic. The woman backed off, the family was upset, and soon after I said my good-byes. I wasn't proud of what I had done, but neither was I repentant.

The next morning, when I ran down the whole happening in prayerful reflection, I found that I still felt both guilty and justified. The woman had acted badly, been a quite real and objective burden. I had acted worse, hurting someone already in pain. She had some excuse for her boorishness. That was clear from her tension, even if I didn't know the exact cause. I had no excuse. My life had very few worries, I had been blessed with a good religious formation, and I was supposed to know myself. So after breakfast I picked up the phone, apologized to my friend, and then apologized to the woman herself. She was quite gracious, making light of the matter and letting bygones go. I hung up with a sigh of relief.

Later I asked myself, in a subsequent reflection: *What have you learned?* The answer seemed to be: *To keep a close watch on my feelings the next time I'm irritated at the dinner table. Better, before I go out to dinner, I should look around inside a bit. I know new people are likely to zero in on my religion or writing. I know they're almost bound to categorize me that way. So I should expect it. In my mind's eye, I should hang loose from the awkwardness it can cause. I should prepare not to squirm if they babble in flattery. I should be ready not to flare if they begin to attack. I should just keep my peace in Christ's Spirit. I'll save myself lots of grief, and maybe even do them some good.*

More often than not, the inside of ourselves, our troubled feelings, holds the clue to what we've made of a recent experience. By going over the tender spots and focusing clearly on the residue that last night's conversation, or yesterday's work, or this morning's waking dread has left, we can come to grips with the here and now. If we are edgy or depressed or blushing before God, right now we are people needing help, wanting a change. If we are peaceful and upbeat, right now all is well. The goal of regular reflection is simply to make more times peaceful and upbeat, more of our life pleasing to our maker.

This means that we shouldn't attend to our feelings as an end in itself. We shouldn't scrape them over endlessly, picking at the scabs. When one is accustomed to religious reflection, a quick survey usually will suffice. As soon as we whistle, our feelings will step forward, like kids in a military school. Giving us their names, they will point to their causes, and to their consequences as well. We shall deal with both causes and consequences later, but here it may be well to illustrate how attention to the inside usually shows one the connections to be pursued.

For example, the guilt and irritation I found the morning after the dinner party were quite straightforward. I didn't have to poke around very much to learn how I felt about my performance. Nor was the connection from my feeling of guilt to its cause roundabout. I had let myself get irritated and take the woman's outburst personally, when in all likelihood it had had virtually nothing to do with me. The woman had been making a statement to relieve her inside pressures; she had been uttering a cry for help. Had I not been so self-centered, so obtuse to what the Spirit likely was asking of me, I probably would have been able to let the flak slide by and focus on the "flaker." The main cause of my guilt, then, was my self-centeredness.

Equally clear were the first consequences. The only decent thing to do was try to repair things with an apology. Fortunately, that seemed to work, restoring the relationships to an even keel. Fortunately, God's forgiveness of us says that we can forgive one another and make new beginnings.

Things to Notice

Sigmund Freud, the father of modern psychology, once said that people are healthy if they can love and work. I find this saying very helpful, for it spotlights two of the most important ingredients of peace of mind. Indeed, taken broadly enough, love and work sum up a majority of our human needs, and a majority of the Spirit's good effects in us. Therefore, they furnish a majority of the things our reflections have to notice.

Love is the deeper and more central issue. In the case of Barbara, her husband's betrayal of her love had thrown her way down in the dumps. In the case of Paul, I always suspected that his drinking camouflaged a fear of intimacy, or a sexual confusion, that caused him terrible pain. In the cases of both, the love of God had not penetrated the core, convincing them that nothing could separate them from their source. More generally, love is nearly always a relevant emotion to consider. If we are not giving and receiving love satisfactorily, we are bound to feel unsatisfied. If the balance of payments between what we do for other people and what we get back in return is lopsided, we are bound to have big problems. And if we are not convinced that God's love has no limits, always wishes our good, we have not secured the foundation of our religious lives.

For Freud *love* implied sex, though of course not simplistically. It is well to look regularly at this implication, if only to learn again that love is bigger than sex. The love between parents and children, for example, has at most a low sexual component. Fathers do relate to daughters differently than to sons. Mothers do vary their reactions according to their children's sex. But the main stream of parental love is protective and nurturing, not erotic. What parents most need from their children is their children's need of them. In fact, the years of maturity (say twenty-five to fifty) are the times when all of us want to take care of "things": little ones, business, the needs of society at large.

It is also well, therefore, to look closely at those we would like to have need us. Our spouses, lovers, children, and friends are the main actors in our life's drama. If they are prospering, we have large reasons for feeling good and thanking God. If they don't appreciate us, we have large reasons for depression. Naming our feelings of depression or satisfaction is the beginning of understanding how our love life is going.

My friend Kathy, for instance, beams eight days out of ten. Big with her third child, she exudes an infectious joy. She doesn't have lots of money. Her job is problematic. But her husband is rock-solid and tender. Her family is healthy and warm. To be sure, some days she is tired and hassled. The bills are big and the kids take a lot of energy. But her central love holds firm, so the new life kicking within her fills her to overflowing. When she says her prayers at the end of the day she finds herself mainly giving thanks.

Naturally, no case like this is as simple as I've made it. My point is merely to underline the major lesson. Here the major lesson seems to be: By and large, the quality of our love determines the quality of our peace of mind. If we can say, with Saint Augustine, "Love, and do what you like," we know the liberty of the children of God.

Work, however, is also important. Unless we are using our time well and can feel we are making a contribution, we are shut off from a second most important source of peace and satisfaction. For, contrary to my friends' relative who hated poetry, we all have a vocation, an inner calling to God, to *poiesis:* making, creativity. Some of us can make things with our hands: houses, chairs, cakes, dresses. Others can make things with their minds: medical diagnoses, classroom presentations, business proposals, legal analyses. And still a third group can make things happen among people: organize political units, run a Girl Scout troop, get together a dinner party, direct a military operation. Whatever our particular kind of talent, we all need to make things work. In fields, factories, kitchens, and offices, unproductive time lies heavy on all hands. To be sure, there is a time for recreation and loafing. We all need free zones and fun. But our deeper need is to be about the work of making. The idle rich are almost in hell.

We also work, of course, to make money. Creativity is not the whole work story. For the sake of family and survival, many people must do work they barely can stomach. They especially might profit from a close look at their feelings. For them especially religious reflection might be very healing. For example, they might discover alternatives to their present situations. They might become more reconciled to God's will if indeed there is nowhere else they can go. Creative hobbies could provide a good outlet. The social side of their work might better compensate them for the drudgery. Whatever the particular problems or solutions, the basic issue stands clear. When we find satisfaction in our work, as when we find satisfaction in our love, we gain large shares of peace of mind.

When Barbara Paid Attention

Barbara began to find peace of mind, contentment in the Spirit, when she started paying attention to her feelings. As long as her feelings controlled her, working at the edges of her awareness, she was a basket case. When she began to stop the hurly-burly, pin an emotion to the board for a careful look, things began to change for the better. This stopping took considerable courage, since she was not sure what she would find. It demanded a first step on a path of honest analysis. She could not be certain where the next steps would lead, whether God would console or chastise. But she had had enough of useless suffering, was sick of her worries and tensions. So she grabbed herself by the scruff of the neck and forced her mind to pay attention, her conscience to open up.

My part in this beginning was mainly to act as a sounding board. I tried to bounce back to her the thoughts, memories, and feelings she was having—to make them objective enough, available enough, that we might start to see them clearly. Because I was less involved, I was less inclined to lose the forest in the trees. Because I was trained in theology, I was better able to point out some of the implications for her faith. Barbara was new at the business of religious reflecting. It took some time for her to sharpen her skills. In the beginning I therefore better saw the main themes of the story she was telling, the basic characteristics of the self she possessed then and there.

The main theme of her first story was her husband's betrayal. Later she shifted to self-confidence and initiative. The basic characteristic of her early self was victimhood. Later she became spunky, excited about new opportunities for growth. In her passover from the first to the second story, she could feel her relation to Christ become adult.

Initially, therefore, Barbara paid most attention to her worst wound: her husband's rejection of her. With many tears and racking sobs she finally put this under the spotlight. What she found was that without her husband's approval she didn't know how to stand. In fact, she felt worthless on several levels: without brains, without charm, without sex appeal. So deep was the threat in her husband's rejection that she forgot huge parts of her story. For instance, she almost completely blocked out what she could do as a nurse, all she accomplished as a mother. She almost completely forgot her never-failing worth in God's eyes. When I first brought forward these other parts of herself, citing them as evidence that her husband's rejection was far from the whole story, she tended to dismiss them. Similarly, when I criticized her husband's character, pointing out that his record hardly qualified him to judge anyone else's worth, she tended to defend him.

But before long the bigger picture began to return. Almost despite herself, she admitted that she was a competent nurse, that men other than her husband found her attractive, that her kids were riding out the storm. In the same way she began to agree that her husband's character was quite faulty, that most of the blame was his. Finally, she began to understand that God's favor does not depend upon our good performance, that we really are saved by grace. After these admissions and agreements, we could move away from her hurts and failures. Thenceforth, we began to stress her strengths.

As it worked out, Barbara was able to improve both her love life and her work. When her husband left, her love narrowed to her boys. In fact, she was in danger of swamping them with affection, possessing them with concern. She first rebroadened her love by lunching regularly with a couple of good women friends. Then, some months later, she joined a group that included single men and began accepting dates. A simple program of reading the Bible helped to stir up her love of God and strengthen her spiritual life. Progress came in her work when she took a refresher course and then a part-time job. Not only did this get her mind off herself, it restored her confidence that she could be of use to many other people. As a result, her later move back East and acceptance of a full-time job bore little fear and trembling. By then she was well on the mend, looking ahead instead of backward.

Because she was able to pay attention to her feelings, stand still and face her here and now, Barbara rewrote her life story, recast her character. When I first met her she thought of herself as a victim, a sufferer in a tragedy. There were good grounds for this, but as a long-term role it was sure to be destructive. So we worked at drawing out the feelings lodged at the sides of her hurt and rejection. These included both anger and hopelessness. The anger was a blessing, for it quickly became positive. Using it, she could assert that she would take no more shabby treatment. The hopelessness began to melt when we found positive things for her to consider, both her own talents and the resources of the gospel. Like lights at the end of the tunnel, thoughts of helpful friends, useful work, the love of God, or a new romance started to lure her forward. As she found things to do, reasons to look ahead, her spirits and spunk picked up. She got a new hairstyle and a few new clothes. She lost several pounds and inches. One day her older boy said she was the best-looking mom in his class; that night she brought home three of the world's biggest ice cream sundaes.

In this positive phase, Barbara noticed other feelings emerging. Like little shoots of green growth, they said her winter was ending. We tried to water them a bit, that they might spread out and cover more ground. We tried to tie them into the religious virtue of hope: expecting a good future from God. Thus we focused on the beauty of the lush foothills, the pleasures of the free concerts, the nourishment of good books. As she realized the positive effects such simple things can bring, their easy availability, and the way that they symbolize the generosity of God, Barbara began to reconceive her story. An early chapter clearly had ended, but another stood ready to begin. In fact, the early one no longer seemed especially interesting. Whole new adventures, new overtures from God, beckoned her to move ahead.

2.

Getting Smart

The Experience of Insight

One of the most helpful books I've ever read is Bernard Lonergan's *Insight: A Study of Human Understanding*. In it the author tries to teach the reader to understand human understanding. That is a very difficult thing to teach, so the book is long and demanding. Still, the core message is quite simple: When we grasp the implications of catching on, getting the point, solving a problem, we take in hand a wonderful tool for understanding ourselves, the rest of the world, and the mystery of God.

So in this chapter I want to move from "paying attention" to "getting smart": understanding understanding. In the last chapter the focus was here and now experiences, especially here and now feelings. In the present chapter, the focus is the light that flashes when we understand, the power of the experience of insight, the way that God's word illumines our minds.

One of Lonergan's best examples of insight is a famous story about the ancient Greek scientist Archimedes. The king had received a present of a gold crown, and he wanted to know whether the gold was pure. So he summoned Archimedes and told him to work out an answer. Archimedes hefted the crown, turned it over, scraped at it delicately. In his mind's eye, he considered it from this angle and that. But the more he worked, the more stubborn the problem became. The king was getting impatient. Archimedes could not melt down the crown. Somewhere there had to be a solution, but as the days passed he was gnashing his teeth in frustration.

To get his mind off the problem, relieve his headache and tension, Archimedes took himself to the public baths. Perhaps a soothing soak would help. As he dawdled in the water, relaxing and letting go, he noticed a block of wood floating by. Funny how some things float and others sink, he thought. Must have something to do with their different densities. And then it struck him: he could set the crown in a tank and compare its displacement of water to that of pure gold. If the results were the same, the crown would have to be pure. If the results differed significantly, the crown would be a fake. All this came to him in a flash. The pieces of the puzzle jumped together and a lightning bolt leaped forth. Seized with delight, Archimedes shouted *Eureka!* ("I've found it!") I picture him bounding from the bath, grabbing his towel, and hightailing it home to test his hypothesis.

Whatever the historical details of the real-life story, Archimedes serves to illustrate the experience of insight. When we have a big problem, and we work on it for a long time, sometimes its solution comes with thunder and lightning. The tension we have built up, the strain and worry, break out like flood waters through a dam, soaking us with excitement and a sense of grace. The experience of insight is a pure joy, a big clue to what human beings are made for. For its sake, scientists spend years and years in lonely laboratories. In its wake, peoples the world over have honored wisdom.

Insight like that of Archimedes is a rare instance; it is much clearer and more powerful than ordinary understanding. The insights that carry us through most of our days are considerably less dramatic. Nonetheless, even they are significantly fulfilling. In fact, the delight we feel in solving a problem—finding a better way to do our taxes or a better technique for baking our bread—is a humble cousin to the joys of prize-winning scientists. But the most significant insights for our purposes here, and the ones most equal to those of major science, are the solutions that change our personal lives, the answers to our deep emotional or religious problems.

I remember receiving a letter that sang with joy because the writers had solved a deep personal problem. A family we knew had moved back to the man's hometown to take over his father's business. At the time of the move it had seemed a good idea, since the business was prosperous and the father had had a mild heart attack. But after a couple of years the whole family was in a deep funk. The man hated the sort of detail the job involved, and his father would not retire. Between having to deal with nuts and bolts and having to put up with his father's interference, his disposition completely soured. He barked at his wife, nagged at the kids, and drove the whole family to seek pastoral counseling.

My wife and I learned a little of this story, in bits and pieces, through casual socializing. The people felt we understood their background so they would talk to let off steam. By the end of an evening we would all be laughing, but of course the basic problem remained. Then we happened not to see the couple for several months, due to busyness, vacations, and the like. One day we got a letter, postmarked Tennessee, and opened it to find our friends apologizing for having left so suddenly. They explained that they had been sitting around one night, going over their troubles for the nth time, when a light dawned. They could simply leave and begin again somewhere else. Like Abraham, the father of their faith, they could wander to make a new start.

So within a week they had told his parents, sold their home, and hit the road for Nashville. The man had always regretted not having gone to law school. The woman was willing to try anything. He enrolled in law school at Vanderbilt, she began to work in real estate, and in their early forties their souls began to breathe again. I'll never forget the happiness and relief that sang in their letter. Having solved such a painful problem, they were as if resurrected or reborn.

The Place of Concrete Details

The center of the experience of insight is the flash of light that floods the mind. Suddenly one sees how the pieces of the puzzle fit together, and the seeing is surprisingly lovely. If we start to analyze insight, however, we find that the flash of light usually has certain preconditions. To be sure, no preconditions can substitute for sheer intelligence or divine grace. People gifted with exceptional brain power or holiness will always have better understanding of the world or God than the rest of us. But there are constants in the experience of insight whose grasp can improve anyone's understanding. If we realize how most solutions to problems occur, we can improve our problem-solving.

In the last chapter we stressed paying attention,

especially to the feelings troubling us. Such attention, we said, was the first step on the road to peace of mind. This chapter is concerned with the second step: solving the problems that we find our feelings presenting us. It does little good simply to realize that, here and how, we are discouraged or feeling guilty. Solid healing only begins when we start to sense ways to free ourselves from our current binds. The main way, of course, is to understand why we are feeling what we are, to grasp the pattern to our emotions. Hence our concern now with understanding.

Fortunately, the stress we placed in the last chapter on paying attention can also help us to get smart. An insight pivots between the concrete details of the problem before us and the pattern that gives those details some sense. So, we help our chances of understanding if we pay careful attention to the concrete details of our problem and seek out quite specifically how the Spirit has been making us feel. We can see this in the example of Archimedes.

Archimedes began trying to understand whether the crown was pure gold by familiarizing himself with the crown's details or special characteristics. He hefted it, turned it over, scraped at it carefully. In that way, he was familiarizing himself with all of its respects, using his sight and touch. Had he thought of it, he might also have used his hearing (struck the crown to find out how it sounded), and even his smell and taste. Whatever he actually did, we can assume that over the days he was working on this problem the crown became very familiar. He probably thought he knew its every feature, probably told his wife he was sick of the fool thing. But in the bath, in a moment of relaxation, he found an aspect he had overlooked. From his unconscious, where parts of him he wasn't even aware of continued to work on the problem,

popped up the feature of *density*. The block of wood
floating by triggered this perception. The crown had a
specific density, by which one could compare it to an
equal volume of gold. Thus density became the key to
the crown's *identity*, what it peculiarly or uniquely
was. With this key the other data fell into a pattern
and Archimedes' problem was three-fourths solved.

In dealing with almost all human problems, it
helps greatly to pay calm, careful attention to concrete details. The more we familiarize ourselves with
every aspect of our puzzle, the likelier we are one day
to solve it. This is true of personal problems as well
as impersonal, of the details of divorces and job
changes as well as the details of physics or accounting
or breadmaking. But in personal problems we often
shy away from studying the details, because so many
of them are apt to be painful. The psyche can block
out things we are not ready to handle (such as
religious implications that seem too stark) so that we
do not go into shock or suffer overload.

Still, once the first pains of a personal problem
have subsided, we are wise to start the process of
examining the details. Trying to be patient, not to
force things too much, we can assemble the different
pieces of the puzzle by dragging out all the thoughts,
actions, and words that might be relevant.

In the case of our friends who finally realized
they could move away, this process took many months.
Their feelings of guilt and frustration were so strong
that they overlooked a quite obvious solution. They
had moved into their present situation easily enough.
Coming to take the job had been no problem. Why
couldn't they move out in the same way, just give
their regrets and take a powder? Because they had so
badly wanted the new job and situation to work.
Because the whole prior history of the man's relation

with his father (the competition, the irritation, the mutual love-hate) had been involved. Because all the pressures created by the man's frustration had made the whole family unable to think clearly, to relax before a God of unlimited possibilities and see things afresh.

However, one night things finally clicked. The people didn't give us all the physical details, but I picture them relaxing, somewhat like Archimedes. Probably it was well into the night, when the kids had gone to bed. Perhaps they had added a couple of logs to the fire. Whatever, their minds were finally free enough to recognize the obvious. The demands they had been making on themselves to stay were not an ultimate obligation. The thoughts they had had that they were too old to start over simply didn't stand up to a firm challenge. Finally they realized that the peace and happiness of the family as a whole were far more important than sticking the job out merely for the sake of their pride. The light dawned, the conflicts washed away, and they were free of their painful chains. Like the Hebrews leaving Egypt, their exodus was a great liberation.

Asking How Things Hang Together

Once we have spread out on the table all the concrete details we can find, the question becomes: How do they hang together? What is the pattern in which they make the most sense? To answer this question, it often helps to move the pieces of the puzzle around, if need be even physically. We should make lists, tables, diagrams—anything that might help us notice the key clue and get a fresh intuition of the pieces' best fit. Insights usually come from good images. When we put together a vivid picture or a striking table of numbers, we give our minds good materials in which to find the answer they seek. The process of understanding is an interplay between a questioning, probing mind and relevant, well-organized data. The good teacher, therefore, is the one who furnishes striking examples, gives the student vivid images in which to see the point of the lesson. The good religious counselor but sets the point of the lesson in the bigger context of God's mystery.

One of the best ways to sift out practical problems and organize their concrete details is to translate the different pieces into numbers. Of course, such a translation has its dangers, so we must be ready to add in things (for example, feelings we suspect come from the Spirit). But assigning numbers to the different aspects of a problem often clarifies the task considerably.

For example, suppose a group of six people have the task of dividing up a certain amount of money according to the quality of each person's work. For the sake of simplicity, let's say that the amount of money is $120,000. In order to solve this problem and reach a decision that will be fair, they might make some simple numerical calculations. For instance, if each person's work were equal in quality and worth to all the others', a simple division of the money into six equal parts would give each person $20,000. Therefore, $20,000 could serve as a basic reference point. A person considerably above average in his or her performance ought to get more than $20,000, and a person considerably below average ought to get less than $20,000.

Few groups are completely equal, however, so in most decisions like this we have to become more precise, breaking the problem-solving process down into its component parts. Let's say that the six people are all college teachers whose job description stresses three principal duties: teaching, research, and community service. If the group could assume that each of these three component parts was equally important, someone might propose a procedure like this: "Let's use an overall scale of twelve points, with a maximum of four points in each of the three categories. Thus a person who is an outstanding teacher will get four points. A person who is fair at research will get two or three points. And a person who has done a minimal amount of community service will get only one point. If all these descriptions were to fit an actual person, Jane Doe, she would have a total of seven or eight points. If, by comparison, Bob Jones came up with a total of nine or ten points, he should receive a bigger share of the $120,000 than Jane Doe."

The main issue, of course, is not any particular scale or way of assigning the numbers. The main issue is taking a complicated matter, which at first glance one does not know how to resolve, and breaking it down into manageable parts. The advantage of translating the parts into numbers is the ease with which numbers can be manipulated. The disadvantage is all the things it's hard to quantify. For example, if Jane Doe is a sweetie who makes everybody's work go easier, while Bob Smith is a crotchety old bear, it won't seem fair to reward Bob more than Jane. The scale or translation device will seem unjust, and so require adaptation.

This reminds us that however we choose to lay out the parts of a problem—by numbers, diagrams, or anything else—the layout must really serve the solution process, not become a sacred cow or take on a life of its own. As the Sabbath was made for human beings, not human beings for the Sabbath, so techniques were made for solving problems, not solving problems for techniques.

Relatedly, we should not make the layout scheme so complicated that people get lost in it or lose sight of the fact that the scheme is only as good as the understandings and decisions it produces. Unless we come up with a good final product, our schematization has been only diddling. In the example at hand, for instance, the point is to come up with a fair distribution of the $120,000. In the example of my friends trying to come to grips with the man's frustrating job situation, the point was a decision that would give each part of the situation its due. Let's try to imagine how my friends might have proceeded more systematically.

Suppose the family had sat down with a number scheme, making a silent prayer that God grant their deliberations a wise outcome. Using a number scheme, they might have clarified their problem by listing each component they thought important and giving it a numerical value. So the good salary of the job might have merited a $+5$, the frustrations of the job a -7. The pain of failing the man's father might have been worth a -4, the relief the family foresaw in getting the father off their backs a $+6$. This would have been a rough analysis, nothing very precise. But it might have helped the people to see the total picture more quickly, shown them the full dimensions of their unhappiness much sooner. If the total score of the present situation had kept coming out a minus, they might have had a bigger prod to make a change.

I must repeat again, however, that getting into the analysis itself is more important than the particulars of any analytic scheme, for the analysis is what really turns on the energies of the mind and produces the solution. Any scheme can be supplemented or revised or set aside. It is only an instrument to help one think clearly and take all God's nudges into account. The analysis is always the crux: persistently asking the data to fall into shape, insisting that they cough up an answer. A prime marvel and blessing of the human condition is that if, like Archimedes, we keep asking, usually we will find an answer. The God who has set us in the midst of a problematic world has given us good tools for coping.

The Shifts That Come with Light

If an insight is significant at all, the light it brings shifts our perspective considerably. For scientists like Archimedes, insights can lead to a whole new theory that sets data such as things' different densities in a fresh, very useful light. Ordinary people in the midst of difficult decisions can find insights converting them—turning their lives around, freeing them from prisons of frustration, giving them hope and new possibilities for pleasing God. Understanding is such a central part of being human that insight is crucial to our development and happiness. Were public education really pivoted on insight, we might see a generation of very happy kids. Were churches, synagogues, and other groups concerned with morality really to love the light, we might see much more justice.

For there are revolutions implied in insight. When one makes understanding a crucial human act, all sorts of conversions or overturnings become possible. These revolutions are not violent or political. Their first impact is completely personal and helpful to peace. Thus Archimedes probably never could look at water or gold again as he had before. Thus my friends who moved to Tennessee got onto a completely different track, ending up happy in southern Texas after the man finished law school.

Insights of any significance are powerful stuff, capable of producing vast changes. That is probably the reason why people who don't want change so strongly oppose both insight and its preconditions: free inquiry, access to information, a theology that encourages questioning. We could name both individuals and groups, foreign and domestic, who fall into this category. The most significant among them for our purposes, however, are the ones we see in the mirror. It is the enemy looking out through our own eyes who does us the most damage.

Let's go back to two earlier cases, my counselee Paul and the angry woman with whom I had the confrontation at dinner. Both illustrate the sickness that spawns when we block the way to insight and refuse to follow the light.

In Paul's case, by refusing to set the data of his drinking in the pattern of alcoholism, he let the whole structure of his life collapse. Facing the facts of his drunkenness, and beyond those facts the causes that lay deep in his psyche or early history, and beyond even those causes the kind of God he had abandoned, was too painful for him even to consider. So his personal life went from bad to worse, increasing his misery. At the time I lost sight of him, he was getting close to the disaster zone. It was not outside the realm of possibility that he would end up a terminal patient in a ward for alcoholics. Having worked on such a ward when I was in the seminary, I had sharp pictures of that kind of end. As I had once held down a terminal alcoholic while doctors drained off two liters of stinking yellow fluids that his ruined kidneys and liver couldn't handle, so one day someone might be holding down Paul. Because they have not been able to face the facts and follow the light, a great many people have missed huge amounts of the peace and joy God had in store for them and have come to very sorry deaths.

Nor were the prospects for the angry woman very cheerful. The rigidity that was taking over her mind, the shrillness entering into her opinions about education, religion, and politics, was getting close to the point of mental illness. One of the signs of mental health is the ability to roll with the punches, be somewhat flexible. When outer pressures or inner demons turn us rigid and take away our ability to laugh at ourselves, we are much less able to cope. One can be very sympathetic to people like the angry woman and Paul, and try to show them great compassion, without denying that their problems are mainly in their heads. Whatever might help them cut loose from their rigid defenses, become more able to follow insight wherever it leads, trust that in making them and the world God has done very good work, would be a great help in their healing. One can't be a healthy human being and stay in flight from the light. Insight, honest pursuit of and response to the light, the drawing by God, is the treasure we've been made for.

In the next section I shall deal more positively with the shifts that come with the light, returning to the happy case of Barbara. Here let me complete the negative picture, for it clarifies all sorts of happenings in both ourselves and the world around us.

In ourselves, we witness a constant battle between openness to the light and closure. Part of this, of course, is simply a matter of limited energy. We don't have the time or strength to follow every lead, examine every pocket of our lifestyle. Getting through the ordinary day at home and work takes most of our resources. So we're all a little less than heroes of light, a little rigid and self-serving. A man like Gandhi shames us all; he rightly was called a *mahatma* ("great soul"). If our small-soulness starts to sour our personality or taint our social relations, however, we really must change it. At that point our closure to the light, our flight from insight, has become significantly destructive. Indeed, it has started to raise the biblical possibility that we hate the light because our deeds are evil (see John 3:20).

In the world around us, unfortunately, that biblical possibility is often a reality. The prison camps of the Soviet Union, the torture chambers of the Latin American dictatorships, the frenzies of slaughter in Southeast Asia, and the terrorisms of Northern Ireland and the Middle East all depend on massive flights from the light, massive fears and hatreds. The similarities at home, in American politics and prison life, fortunately are more muted. Nonetheless, no one who loves insight and integrity has any grounds for complacency about the American political scene. Our past willingness to do violence to huge classes of people— blacks, women, ethnic minorities, the poor—is all too amply documented. Our present unwillingness to understand the consequences of nuclear arms holds the whole world in thrall.

When Barbara Got Smart

When Barbara started paying attention to the details of her situation, asking how they hung together, she took up the life of honest religion, the adventurous pursuit of the light. Rather soon, her efforts began paying off with significant insights, and her life started to shift onto a better track. Although her fears at first outweighed her pleasures, before long she began to love the light. In sketching some of her progress, I mainly hope to encourage others to follow her example.

Naturally, the details of Barbara's ten-year marriage were many. In the beginning, we decided to concentrate on those surrounding her husband's rejection, since they were closest to her biggest pains. At the very start, therefore, Barbara had to make a large commitment in terms of courage. We were going for the biggest troubles and that might have meant radical surgery. Actually, it did not, for the objective details of her husband's rejection turned out to be quite benign. They were much more a matter of his interpretation of Barbara than of her real person or performance. Still, she did not know this at the beginning, so her willingness to pay attention and probe was quite brave.

The details that stood out clustered around her husband's charge that she was stupid and unimaginative. Looking carefully at them, we immediately ran into data that didn't fit. For instance, when I asked Barbara what grades she had received in school, she said Bs and B + s. When I asked how she got along in most social groups, she said she did quite well. And this was confirmed in our own interactions. Barbara had no trouble getting the point of what I was saying, understanding what was going on, or seeing the religious implications. Perhaps, therefore, it was a special sort of "stupidity" her husband had in mind?

Testing this possibility, we started to uncover suggestions that it was indeed. The husband moved in a fast lane, dealing with young executives and advertising types. Their conversation was quick and in-group, full of supposed wit and local references. Barbara didn't know most of the situations to which their conversations referred, and she was not especially articulate. So she became quite shy in the presence of her husband's friends, seldom saying much. I asked her why she thought this displeased her husband so much, since he must have known she wasn't very verbal or witty. She said she guessed it was because he couldn't show her off, take pride in her, impress his fellow-workers and friends. Was that a tendency of his, to show off his spiffy possessions? In fact it was. His need for a flashy car, a huge stereo, and tailor-made clothes had put big holes in their bank account. A large part of his "religion" was serving mammon.

So we came to understand that "stupid and unimaginative" was as much, probably more, in the eye of her husband than in the person of Barbara herself. However, this didn't seem to bring Barbara the comfort I thought it should have, so I played a hunch and pushed for a little more. Barbara certainly was pretty, but had the string of her husband's affairs been connected with sexual dissatisfactions? Did the "stupidity and lack of imagination" tie into sexual fantasies parallel to her husband's desires for a fancy car and tailor-made clothes? I hated to get into this, for all sorts of reasons, but the light of the previous insights seemed to point in this direction. More pieces of the puzzle might fall into place if we could link the affairs to the "stupidity."

We could make the link. Tearfully, Barbara went over some of the bedroom details and recalled that she had not been able to play the games her husband wanted, was put off by the whorish role he often asked. She did indeed not have the "imagination" for that, never could find a way to make it playful rather than degrading. Because this failure had hurt her badly, she had largely repressed it. When we dragged it out for honest study, it (like so many other reptiles) mainly slunk away.

I pointed out that it takes two to play successfully. Both partners have to find the game decent fun. If initially they don't, they have to talk out their differences and help one another adjust. This process, to be sure, can be frustrating. It's always nicer when agreement comes in a flash. But the process also can become a way of growing. Friends or spouses who work through hard problems emerge on the other side much closer, much more aware of their mutual vulnerability and need of God's love.

Because she could be honest and courageous, Barbara quickly "got smart." By this phrase I don't mean that she became cynical or worldly-wise. I just mean that she entered a new phase of maturity, gained a more realistic view of herself and today's world. What she found was some naïveté on her part and some sickness on the part of today's world. By contemporary standards, she was a little inhibited. By the dictates of common sense, Christian faith, and beautiful marriages, many of her husband's notions were selfish and distorted. Barbara emerged from examinations such as these a little rueful, but quite encouraged overall. There were things she perhaps should have known (her prior refrain of "I could have been more understanding" was, looking backward, a clue), but her husband's demands and lack of understanding suggested much selfishness and immaturity on his part. In this light, she felt considerably less rejected, considerably more a person of solid worth. In this light, the breakup of her marriage did not mean her sorry failure before God.

3.

Being Realistic

Bright Ideas and Realities

We have been tracing the frontiers of human wisdom, studying how to pay attention, sharpen our intelligence, and gain a better sense of how God's light tends to move our minds and hearts. If one puts away distraction and attends to matters at hand, there comes a large sharpening of focus. Similarly, if one puts a whip to one's brain and forces it to ask how the data fit together, there comes a large leap in brain power. Understanding is the act that occurs frequently in those who pay attention and discipline their brains. Stupidity is the fate of those who cannot focus and will not think. God is not a lover of stupidity.

Understanding, however, does not yield reality or truth plain and simple. For that one must reflect and judge. When Archimedes jumped from the bath he had a bright idea that *might* have been workable. Only when he actually had made it work did he know for sure that it was true. Just as the road to hell is paved with good intentions, so the number of useless bright ideas is legion. My friend who is always scheming to make money has at least one eye-popping insight a week. First it was disposable blood-analysis kits, to take advantage of the growing interest in fitness. ("In every home a vampire," I uncharitably thought.) Then it was selling irresistible household items using his home as his office. Then his wife made the easy leap to the pink cadillacs to be earned by selling cosmetics door to door. Another week and they were on to sponsoring package tours to the Holy Land. Seldom have I seen such a fertile financial intelligence. Virtually never did it produce a project two Cub Scouts or Brownies would have trusted.

The difference between what might be so and what is very likely to be so is the difference between hypothesis and solid theory. In the interval between the creative notion that Archimedes came up with and his surety that the notion would work occurred several very thorough testings. We call this testing process *verification,* and it is not limited to scientists.

For example, the prudent among us do some thorough research before they pour their money into home blood-letting, their time or hopes into money-making schemes. They ask God to detach them from greed and false worries about money. They go over the process in which they gained their bright idea, testing whether the flash of insight did really make sense of the data. They open the search to the possibility of new data: other ways to predict the future of the current interest in fitness, household products, or cosmetics. If they are shrewd and honest, they put a big stop sign in front of the passions that may be driving them in their investigations (in these cases, the ardent desire to make money). If they are experienced and prudent, they leave big margins for safety. If they are faith-filled, they keep chanting, "It is easier for a camel to go through the eye of a needle than for a rich man to enter the kingdom of God" (Matt. 19:24).

Reality, the wise among us know, is not a matter of our mere wishing. Barbara wished with all her heart that the reality of her marriage would be rosy. Looking at her two handsome children, her tidy little house, her quite acceptable face in the mirror, she thought that all had to be well. So the lipstick on her husband's collar, the strange patches of unaccounted time in her husband's schedule, and the irritation that seemed always to lurk beneath her husband's surface were shunted to the side. These further data, other considerations that should have been factored, she had to blink away. The result was quite a long period of unrealistic living, years and years of dreaming.

On the whole, unrealistic living is a sorry bargain. We may in times of special stress have to indulge what we want to be the case, but over the long haul only living by what really is the case is satisfying. For almost always a part of us knows what really is the case, even when a larger part of us won't admit it. The result is an inner division, making for great conflict and unease. On the surface we may continue to chatter and sparkle. In our depths we are suffering a dark night. Society gives us so much schooling in surface living that we can chatter and sparkle for months. Religion would force us to go beneath our brittle chatter, so genuine religion can seem an enemy. We may go to church and mouth pious sentiments, but our hearts are far from God. The real God is a truth-teller, demanding worship in spirit and truth. Thus the real God is a breaker of brittle surfaces, a critic of merely hypothetical living.

In *The Clouds*, one of the comedies of the ancient Greek playwright Aristophanes, Socrates has his head in the clouds. Using the prejudices of the common populace, Aristophanes pokes fun at the wisest man in Athens, suggesting that philosophers seldom have their feet on the ground. The truth, of course, is just the reverse of this common prejudice. The genuine lover of wisdom is attentive, intelligent, and absolutely judicious. From long experience or rich endowment, wise, truly religious women and men want passionately to deal with what is real. They know that hypothetical living is a bad bargain, a cheat and a serious enemy.

So Barbara, who had a bent for wisdom, slowly confronted the brittleness she saw in her mirror, finally let her deeper disquiet speak out the truth. Wisdom comes through suffering, the greater Greek playwright Aeschylus knew. It is through the cracks in superficial living that we fall into the hands of the living God. As long as we are all rush, brightness, and bluster, the Spirit of God can do little for us. Only when, like the Chinese philosopher Lao-tzu, we become dark and empty, in need of heartier fare, can the Spirit of God begin our healing and start to mature us in spirit and truth.

Reflective Understanding

Wise people are those who have good judgment. Good judgments are the expressions of accurate acts of reflective understanding. In this section we try to illustrate reflective understanding.

Direct understanding or insight is a matter of grasping the form or meaning in the data we have been pondering. Archimedes shouted "Eureka!" because he had grasped how the data on the crown might fit together. Reflective understanding is a grasp of what Lonergan calls a "virtually unconditioned." By "unconditioned" he means something that no longer depends on anything else. In the case of Archimedes' crown, the truth of the hypothesis depended on more testing. When Archimedes had assured himself, through thorough experimentation, that he had verified his hypothesis, he understood that his idea was not just bright but solid, not just possible but true. In that reflective understanding, the conditions or dependencies or qualifications attending his theory fell away. No longer was his notion of the uses of the displacement of water just conditional. Having been thoroughly verified, it was absolutely true, completely independent of other suppositions or assumptions.

Well, not *completely* independent, because nothing in the created, contingent order is. All theories and other works of human beings, as all human beings themselves, are dependent upon their Creator, conditioned by the divine will and power that let them be and keeps them existing in this complex world of interconnections. Thus any act of reflective understanding discovers or asserts only a *virtually* unconditioned. It is as though (prescinding from the dependence on God) the theory of hydraulic displacement were truth pure and simple. For the purposes of practical projects like weighing the king's crown (and saving his own neck), Archimedes' judgment was absolutely valid.

In the more commonsensical matters that preoccupy most of the rest of us, reflective understanding usually has to do with less precise virtually unconditioneds. Human affairs are more subtle, murky, and emotion-laden than scientific experiments of weighing things in water. So my friend stalking a kill in business has to deal with more iffy propositions. Still, his business acumen will improve, and his bank account prosper, in the measure that he too becomes more carefully reflective. If he goes over his possible projects in a careful way, rechecking the data and getting help from God to bottle up his greed, he will be more likely to invest in the good bets and keep himself free of the bad. So, for example, he may find a second kind of home chemistry kit, suitable for determining pregnancy, diabetes, and other diseases, as well as the indices of physical fitness. This, in all likelihood, would be a better product to back. Or he may realize that all of his prospects are harebrained and his financial hopes better realized by safe bonds at lower rates. Finally, he may come to blush at his headlong rush after money and consider the lilies of the field. The point is that as his reflective understanding grows more powerful, his demand for the fulfillment of relevant conditions more insistent, his judgments will become more reliable.

I remember discussing a painful move with a long-time academic friend. He had left one troubled situation and been two years in another that had beckoned as a much better place. However, slowly—and to his deep distress—the new situation was also proving unacceptable. Promises made when the new place had been wooing him fell flat and were disregarded. Duties never mentioned in the original job description came floating in from left field. The colleagues he had assumed would be open showed themselves intractably stuck in the mud. Finances he had been led to expect turned out to be funds he would have to raise himself. So, once again, the man had to review his past experiences and future options. He felt guilty, stupid, and abused. But his drive to honesty was such that he was willing to reenter the reflective test-tunnel and once again lay bare his soul to God.

First he checked back on the original data: the offer made to him and his own original dispositions. In hindsight, the offer had been vaguer than he had thought, more dependent on goodwill in the offerers than on the strict letter of the contract. Similarly, his own need to leave the prior bad situation probably had given him a rose-colored view of the new. True, friends counseled him not to be too hard on himself, or think he could have known then what he had learned in the past two years. But he dicated a memo to himself for the future: Seldom make a deal that depends on the generosity of the contractors. Always write into the agreement very explicitly the terms you have to have.

Second, my friend went into his own character. Was he the sort of person doomed always to be dissatisfied? Was it, perhaps, not the times and places that were out of joint but his own demanding psyche? This was a hard question to pose, of course, because if the answers started coming in affirmatively he would have to face some wholesale changes in his personality. Fortunately, his most demanding self-analysis turned up only negative answers. No, he was not a chronic complainer, an inveterate malcontent. In earlier jobs he had been quite content. Had the colleagues in these past two jobs been normally truthful, good to just the average degree, his work and peace probably would have prospered. The objective facts seemed to indicate that he had come into an unusual run of bad luck, which (in the case of the second job) his psychic needs might have caused him to under-anticipate but he could in no way have predicted. So he judged that the second situation was objectively bad, which made trying to leave it not only sensible but the likely will of God.

Self-Criticism

Of the two moments in my friend's reflective survey, the second was the deeper. The details he

reviewed were important enough, but his own character was the profound issue. For the details in any
reflective understanding usually are rather distant from,
or external to, the self. It is the person viewing the
data, grasping their form in insight and musing out
their significance who is the center of the drama. That
is why writers of maxims such as La Rochefoucauld
have noted that, while many of us complain about our
memories, few of us complain about our judgments.
Our judgments are our selves. To have bad judgment
is to have a bad self: stupid, unrealistic, or biased.
The irony is that the judgmental process itself, were
we to understand, deepen, and sharpen it, would
greatly mature our selfhood. In the reflective survey
that judgment naturally entails, the judger and the
mystery of God are the most important items.

Take the two friends I have been using, the
would-be entrepreneur and the unfortunate academic.
The first, overall, is a person of at best average
maturity or depth. He is young, so life may deepen
him considerably, but at the moment he generally
lives close to the surface. So he impresses the typical
observer as energetic, bright, and ambitious. He speaks
quickly, makes pleasant jokes, and loves to get things
cracking. Little in him withdraws for second opinions.
He is seldom notably in repose, at least in public.
Thus it is not surprising that he keeps stumbling into
silly projects. He has yet to gain the discipline needed
to reach the depths of a calmly objective self.

My second friend is quite different—older and
more reserved. It was in character for him to go over
his painful recent history, very like him to consider
his own possible failings. He is not used to making
bad judgments, because since his youth he has always
reviewed the ways he has gone wrong. (Generally it
is not typical of the wise person to bang her head

against the same closed door again and again. Wisdom may come to her through suffering, but she does her best to shorten the time of pain.) Thus when my friend the academic finally concluded that most of the cause of his bad judgment and decision had lain outside his essential self, he could rest content with his verdict. Having found the few places where he could do better in the future, and having looked hard at his own basic disposition, he could move on to new situations and decisions, confident that his main machinery was in good order and that the rest lay in the hands of God.

It is hard to overestimate the importance of this confidence, and of the regular self-criticism which alone validly can produce it. When we are not confident that our main machinery—our faculties for dealing with things as they actually are—is in good order, we suffer a deep distress. Usually we are not very familiar with this machinery, but the worse likelihood is that we don't want to become familiar. So we treat life like a rat's maze: a series of strange turnings we must get through by trial and error. And we tend to imitate a rat's agitated, jittery sort of running, as though more speed would mean better passage.

The best way to remedy this dysfunctional state of affairs is to learn the machinery that drives us. Through good counsel, reading, or solitary tramps by the light of the moon, we must begin the trip to our center. Insofar as the most frequent trigger to this trip is the pain of previous bad judgments, the "criticism" that judgmental reflection entails does imply some hard sayings to the self. We the presiding officer have to give us the hang-dog offender a thorough talking-to. But it doesn't help to do this in a haranguing, abusive fashion, and it is pernicious to turn it into a florid symphony on the theme of "You're no damn good." No, the best way is simple, straightforward, and slightly humorous: "You really botched it this time, my idiot. Good for the humility, but tough on the nerves."

This was the tone Barbara and I slowly were able to find. In the beginning she not only did not know herself well, she was sizably scared to look. If she had had, in her high school days, to list the ten worst evils that could befall a woman, divorce would have been high up on the list. So entering the process in which she herself became a major item for review took, as I have said, a big dollop of courage. As is often the case, however, she found that some good news counterbalanced the bad. Her survey did not turn up only stupidities and biases. In all honesty she found there had been moments when she had fully suspected what was really going on and that there had been powerful extenuating circumstances.

The foremost of her extenuating circumstances had been the children she wanted so desperately to protect. In retrospect, much of her tardiness in coming to grips with the bad vibrations between herself and Jack had come from the drag of the two kids. She did not want to open what could be a Pandora's box and seriously imperil their future. Her tacit judgment had been that keeping up superficial appearances, outward normality, was very important to their thriving. But in the quiet aftermath, when the most feared eventuality had come to pass and so no longer could skew the assessment process, Barbara saw that her tacit judgment had also been a way of avoiding much of her own fear and self-ignorance. Treating this as lightly as we could, screwing our faces in wry smiles, we noted that she might at that point have lived only about 40 percent of her years and so could hope for a lot of chances to redeem herself.

Good Judgment

It is easy enough to find bad judgments—a trail of wreckage all too helpfully points the way. Good judgment is more hidden, as is overall good health. When we are in good health, we don't think very much about our bodies. They are doing their work, chugging along; so we can attend to our works, friends, and pleasures. But let so small a member of the corporation as the little toe turn up bruised or infected and a whole new consciousness takes hold. As we limp around the corner, curse at the clumsy dog, we realize what Paul had in mind when he spoke of the need for all the members of the church to be in good health. One sore toe can dominate an entire weekend. One captain of industry suffering gout can threaten the economy. And so it is with infections and bruises of the spirit. A person black and blue with envy will have a hard time making good judgments. People cowed by fear or roiled by lust are notorious for their destructiveness.

Good judgment, then, is at least the absence of debilitating spiritual injuries. It depends on a sufficient distance from vice, and a sufficient possession of virtue, to let the judge view the proceedings dispassionately. More positively, however, good judgment is the result of deep self-knowledge, a major gift of the Holy Spirit. When, despite Aristophanes' caricatures, Socrates received the palm of the Delphic oracle and was proclaimed the wisest man in Athens, it was because he of all the citizens best *knew himself*. That was the criterion and advice of the oracle: Know thyself.

Socrates thought his selection strange, because he mainly knew how much he didn't know, but later he realized that the right sort of nescience (or not-knowing) can be positive. Because he didn't claim to know what he did not know, didn't call himself an expert when he was a bumbler, he went to the head of the Athenian class. All around him people were puffing themselves up and pretending to understandings they did not in fact possess. When Socrates punctured their balloons, showing that they had little handle on what they were talking about, they reacted with an anger close to fury. How dare he strip them to the buff, expose their mental nakedness in public! The death he suffered at the end of his career was largely the result of this widespread fury. (In the parallel case of Jesus, the people responsible for the crucifixion could not stand a goodness so much better than their own.)

Socrates dared to reveal the ignorance of his fellow citizens for at least two significant reasons. (He may, of course, have enjoyed deflating their pompous egos, but that was not significant.) The service of the truth was one significant reason, and it was his major motivation. He had studied the city-state long enough to realize that there could be no social prosperity, no genuine commonweal, as long as most of the citizenry were unrealistic. On matters of fact, matters of philosophical outlook, and matters of virtue, the majority of his contemporary Athenians had their heads in the sand. Worse, they did not even know how blinkered and sullied they were.

But what sort of common life can people develop when their premises are woefully out of kilter? How can a good social life result from vice or ignorance? The pursuit of truth, which entailed the naming and stigmatizing of error, was for Socrates a matter of civic duty. To repay the maternal city-state that had given him most of his culture, he had to publish hither and yon the way things actually were.

A second significant reason behind Socrates' political courage was his inner confidence. Apparently he did know himself quite well and so was not afraid to deal with other people in full openness. Since he was not fooling himself with tales either tall or tawdry, he did not have to try to fool his fellow Athenians.

How often we find the reverse of this Socratic inner confidence. Again and again, we find people droning in our ears because they are trying to talk themselves into existence. So foreign are their insides to them, so unfamiliar their minds and consciences, that unless they whip up foam on the surface they doubt there is an ocean. The truth, of course, is that the oceanic depths of any of us are an awesome mystery. If scientists have to deal in billions of light years to map the astral universe, depth-psychologists have to deal in millions of items of memory, virtually infinite combinations and interactions of emotions.

Socrates had a handle on this inner world. Most of his detractors and enemies did not. He could be an honest, courageous critic because he had been to his depths and emerged unafraid. They had to dissimulate and join in cowardly intrigues because they feared the unknown depths within them. The lesson is clearest in the famous thesis of the Johannine political science: "Every one who does evil hates the light, and does not come to the light, lest his deeds should be exposed (3:20)."

Good judgment loves the light, because its deeds are good. It realizes it is ever liable to error, bias, and stupidity. It knows not all its deeds are simon-pure. But it realizes that its call from God to the light is more significant than its vulnerability to the light's enemies. The value of a good conscience—an ability to stand in the light and let the chips fall where they may—outweighs all the passing advantage that shading the truth, pretending to knowledge or virtue one doesn't possess, and the other social dishonesties are ever likely to bring. At the center of good judgment is good conscience, a person in love with the light, a person open to God.

Barbara Comes Together

As Barbara learned the process from attention through intelligence to judgment, she knit her previously frayed personality back together. Attention was not a great problem: she had a woman's keen eye for detail. Intelligence also came into its own, once she learned to discipline her mind and patiently probe the data. Reflection, however, came harder, and so was a more significant victory. Neither her education nor her church-going had given Barbara much training in reflection. She had not been much exposed to meditative musing or quiet contemplation. At first, therefore, the reflective exercises we undertook seemed foreign and difficult. Surprisingly quickly, however, Barbara realized that reflection was something she long had been looking for. When she came to correlate it with the solitary walks she used to take along the beach, her love of the peace of the early morning, she saw that meditation and contemplation are not esoteric but natural. In any healthy, shrewd education or church life, they would have stood front and center.

This proved true of both parts of the judgmental process, the reflective survey of previous hypotheses and the deeper examination of her own biases. As the body naturally wants time to assimilate the nourishment it takes in, so the mind and spirit want peace for assimilation. Prior to her deliberate entry on a spiritual regime, Barbara had been taking in all sorts of data but not processing or digesting them well. The demands of her work and family life had eaten up almost all of her time and energy, leaving her with an agitated, sour center-of-the-mind. The simple introduction of a half hour of quiet morning and night soothed this spiritual upset. In two weeks Barbara was hooked on her periods of regular reflection, addicted positively like an aerobic runner.

In the morning she could come to grips with the beckoning day, get a hold on her tasks and channel her energies. Whereas previously she had bounded from her bed to get breakfast and rush the kids off to school, she found that rising forty-five minutes earlier, slowly waking up with coffee and a view of the dawn, put her in a much better mood. Before long she realized that early morning often is a good time for problem solving. Through the night we regularly wrestle unawares with the symbols of our troubles. In the early morning, before busyness narrows our consciousness, often we can crack the code of these symbols, find what our subconscious has been trying to tell us. For Barbara many times this amounted to but a slight shift in how she regarded her situation. Once, for example, it struck her that although many things in her life were not as she might have wished, many more—good health, good work, wonderful kids— were better than what she had any right to demand from God. Another time it struck her that the crime and disorder dominating the news depend on a background or context of peace and order. If three hundred people in her city were victimized each day, four hundred thousand managed rather well. A third time she realized that though her job payed her less than she knew it ought to by rights, she still enjoyed a standard of living better than three-quarters of the world's 4.5 billions.

These early morning musings yielded not so much practical answers to the hard questions the new day was posing as small shifts in the stance she would take. In general they set troublesome data in a bigger and more positive context. As though the quiet of the early morning offered a border to the noise of the noonday devils, she found her sense of the beauty and gratuity of life expanding to cushion her against its grinding assaults. By planning her way around some of these assaults and preparing her strategy for those she could not avoid, Barbara began to launch her days more confidently. And, because well begun *is* half done, she began to finish her days with more satisfaction.

At night, after the kids had gone to bed, she would give herself a second dose of reflective quiet. Dropping the television-viewing and pulp-reading she previously had indulged, she started to make doing the dishes or listening to good music or swinging on the porch a mode of settling down. Through a quiet review of the day her troubles became less threatening. If the morning tended to present the day as a series of challenges, the night tended to summarize the day as a course of hurdles successfully run. She could note the places where she had nicked a hurdle because she had come to it off stride. She could sense a tug of sadness in having to put another of her limited number of days to bed. But mostly she could feel her cares dropping away, as she swung beneath the distant stars. She grew smaller, less important, part of a bigger scheme. So her hopes flowed out to the Creator of the whole, and her guilts were relativized.

The self Barbara came to know as she reflected through the nights emerged as a quite poignant and lovable friend. Some of this feeling, she knew, easily could become sentimental. But more of it was just the slow spread of the wonder that grows with reflection.

We are simply people, and our lives are short. The span of what we run into, when we start to reflect on our days, is vast and embraces much more than just us humans. When we glimpse the space of the starry heavens, the law within us also grows more wondrous and more subtle. This was the philosopher Immanuel Kant's summary of the marvels of the universe: the starry heavens above and the moral law within. After she began reflecting regularly, Barbara felt her anxieties lessen, her core-self center and gain strength. She felt her gratitude to God deepen and her acceptance of her crosses grow firm.

4.

Being Responsible

From Good Judgment to Brave Action

The terminus of judgment is an assertion or a negation. Having pored over the data and our previous understandings, having checked our judgmental capacities and biases, we affirm or deny the hypothesis formed in direct understanding. Thus Archimedes terminated his testing process by asserting the theory of hydraulic displacement. My friend the academician came to rest in the judgment that the disorder in his situation was mainly not his fault. Through her early mornings and late nights or reflective quiet, Barbara came to the point where she could, indeed had to, affirm her own ability to cope with her problems.

In each case, a conclusion or sense of rightness brought the reflective survey to a natural end. These people all continued musing and contemplating, since all had other fish to fry. But regarding the particular problems we have used as instances of judgmental reflection, they all stopped when they found their virtually unconditioneds. Failing the appearance of new data or insights, they had to assert the truth or falsity that their judgmental researches had turned up.

The assertions and denials of judgment are not,

however, the end of the dynamics of consciousness. As we feel an inward pressure to move beyond mere bright ideas to solid judgments, so we feel an inward pressure to put our solid judgments into practice. For Archimedes this meant giving his verdict to the king and putting his theory to work on other physical problems. For my friend the academician it meant engaging the gears of the machinery that would remove him from his unhappy situation. For Barbara it meant taking the first steps in building a new life away from the shambles of her failed marriage with Jack. Because each of these people did in fact swing into action, each followed through on the yield of his or her judgmental reflections and became more whole, not just a speaker of the truth but a courageous doer.

One cannot assert a reality and then live on as though nothing significant has happened. To say that something is, or is not, true and then practically disregard it is to cripple both one's consciousness and one's conscience. One's consciousness—general awareness—presses toward greater and greater transcendence: more facts, sharper understandings, more solid judgments, fuller enactments of such judgments. Just as it frustrates consciousness to stop at the animal level of mere gazing, refusing to pass beyond vision to knowing the significance of what one is seeing, so it frustrates consciousness when we refuse to make our judgments practical. As well, it frustrates conscience, our faculty of moral awareness. Perhaps the primary law of conscience is that our doing should parallel our knowing. When we act against what we know to be the case, or act as though we could ignore what we know to be the case, we develop a bad conscience and soon begin to rationalize. Not wanting to make our doing conform with our knowledge of what is really so, we start to change our knowledge.

An easy example would be a matter of personal behavior such as smoking. If we know that the scientific data and interpretations make a strong case that smoking seriously injures our health, we have the obligation in conscience to give up smoking. (All the minor premises that would have to be added in, such as our obligation to preserve our health, are easily intuited and not worth belaboring here.) However, if we do not want to give up smoking, we easily dispute the scientific data or bracket its relevance to us.

The demand for symmetry between our knowing and our doing is a basic postulate in all areas of ethics. If the ecological data make a solid case that our current ways of treating the planet are systematically fouling it, we have an obligation to change our current ways of treating the planet. Parallel judgments about the international distribution of wealth would call for a change in macroeconomics, about the perils of the buildup of nuclear arms would lead to shifts in political behavior.

The point is not to oversimplify judgments that often can be quite complicated. The point is to stress the connection between judgment and brave action. When we reach relative certainty (a virtually unconditioned) about any state of affairs, we incur the responsibility of letting this conviction shape our action in the sphere of that state of affairs. Many practical questions about tactics can still remain. Two people can reach the same general conclusion that the nuclear arms buildup is crazy and must be opposed, yet differ in how they decide concretely to enact their opposition. What they cannot in good conscience do is reach the judgment about craziness-and-need-to-be-opposed and then sit back apolitically. Somehow—by marching, writing to members of congress, spreading the word to other voters, educating their children, supporting financially people who quit the arms industries—they must become doers of the truths they have judged.

If they do not become such doers, an inner worm begins to ruin their apple. The brightness of good conscience fades and in its place comes a tarnishing cynicism. The vice of this has many aspects, but the one most relevant to our purposes is cowardice. For while sloth is always an enemy, cowardice is the bigger threat to our not following through on the judgments we have formed. As pure judgments, they lie between us and God (the source of our spiritual light). As judgments enacted, followed through upon, they enter the public arena and become social entities. Because a great many people will not stand behind their judgments publicly, for fear of what their neighbors will think or do, a great many people become mere opinionators, personalities of little substance.

Feelings Revisited

The worm of bad conscience produces many negative feelings, both in the individuals who will not match their knowing with brave doing and in the people who suffer from such individuals' inconsistency. In the inactive individuals, the minimal penalty is a sense of division or incompleteness, while a solid self-loathing can mature. People who know in their bones that they are cowards find it hard to love themselves. Not loving themselves, they tend not to love the world or other people. Inverting the biblical injunction, they tend to hate their neighbors as they hate themselves. Since their own houses are places they despise, the "houses" of other people—lifestyle of the people next door, the way the place they work operates, motivations of public figures (not excluding their own ministers)—also become things to be torn down. Since they have to live in a shack, no one else should enjoy a clean and pleasant cottage.

In the people who suffer from the inconsistency of others the minimal reaction is a loss of respect. Again and again we find subordinates losing heart because their superiors have become timid do-nothings. In institution after institution idealism dims because fine words find little match in brave doings. Some of this, of course, spotlights the lifelong task of gaining one's own sense of what is possible in human affairs. Some slippage between ideals and practice seems, on the historical record, well-nigh inevitable. But the analysis that makes human nature so vitiated that we should never expect a brave follow-through is, to my mind, the worst piece of cynical trash. More often than not it simply exonerates the lazy and the cowardly, among whom the person proposing the analysis usually has a quite high profile.

No, the traditional Christian interpretation of human nature—weak but by God's grace capable of being divinized—is the much healthier position. For while it fully confesses that any health in us depends on our Creator's goodness, it takes the Genesis doctrine of the goodness of creation and the New Testament story of grace's abounding over sin as strong encouragements to a brave personal performance.

Thus the feelings that well up when we do not do the good we know we should are healthy and trustworthy. The loathing that a bad conscience brings is meant for the reform of the inconsistency that produces it. On the other hand, the serenity, peace, and joy of a good conscience are equally healthy and trustworthy. When we ring true to ourselves and others, we should enjoy our harmony. This may never be presumptuous. Always it must bow to the mystery of God. But it can and should be enjoyed—offered to

God as one of the graces for which we most passionately give thanks.

To study the link in one's own life between judgment and action, one can take up the witness of one's conscientious feelings. Looking calmly and soberly at one's guilts or depressions, one can probe whether they are valid or off-base. There is such a thing as valid, objectively warranted guilt feelings. Hard as an overly psychologically analyzed society may find it to accept, people should feel bad when they act badly, or when they refuse to act as they should. Such bad feelings are the only inner clue we have to how the Spirit would have us develop. When we pursue the Spirit's peace of mind, we follow the spoor of joy and sadness. Sadness—guilt, depression, inner division, hopelessness—is an important sign, both to those who are immoral and to those who actually have been working hard to live up to their faith's ideals.

To those who are immoral—violent, greedy, disordered in their sexual lives, regular breakers of the Ten Commandments—inner sadness is a clear call to repentance. "Turn back, foreswear your foolish ways," the Spirit says, "because until you do you will have no inner happiness." To those who have been working hard to live up to their faith's ideals, above all the ideals of loving God with whole mind, heart, soul, and strength and loving their neighbors as themselves, sadness is a mode of purification. The Spirit is asking them to detach themselves from worldly pleasures and securities, so that they may be led deeper into divine love.

Joy also functions importantly but differently for the immoral and the hard-trying. The immoral tend to find their joys becoming grosser and grosser. When greed or cruelty becomes habitual, the depraved person can only find happiness in heinous acts of sin.

The unspeakable crimes of the Nazis would be a good illustration—and a vivid prefigurement of hell. The moral—those seriously trying—should consider their peace of mind, their deep inner joy, a major encouragement of God's Spirit. There *is* a peace which surpasses the world's understanding. There is a joy, as C.S. Lewis has taught a great many, that comes as a surprise, a special love letter from God.

Studying their feelings of sadness and joy, people of ordinary moral effort, ordinary ethical goodness, can find a way of progress open up in front of them. "Do the deeds that bring you peace and joy," the Spirit of God is saying. "Follow through on what you know to be true, have judged to be right, and I will increase your solid satisfaction. I do not promise you a rose garden. The joy and peace of God will have their price. But once you've known them you will find this price almost measly, since they will seem a hundredfold improvement over the joyless life you led before."

The Lure of the Future

When the Spirit opens a path that promises growth, saying that the bread crumbs of joy can take us to the desirable castle, our hope is stirred and the future becomes alluring. Hope is the theological (God-given) virtue that allows us to regard the future confidently, expectantly. Without distracting us from the present and drawing off the energies we should give to the problems of today, hope whispers that tomorrow may be beautiful. As any who have ever dreaded tomorrow know, such hope is not to be assumed lightly or evaluated as cheap. Think of all who sit in prisons, with virtually no hope that tomorrow will be a blessing. Political prisoners in dictatorships, spiritual prisoners in dungeons of madness or sin—all tend to recoil from tomorrow; they have to labor mightily to retain their hope. Only those with good work on their minds and warm love in their hearts can face the future expectantly.

The link between the lure of a good future and brave action is not hard to estimate. When we think that the future is open, that things can be turned around or pushed significantly forward, we have a great incentive to brave action. With little standing between our judgments and their execution, we can shift right into strong deeds. Having judged, for example, that things are a mess at the office, we can start the clean-up process, expecting that a few days of hard work will make a great difference. Or, to introduce another wrinkle, having determined that our marriage is getting into rough waters, we can start frank discussions and generous offers to shoulder needed changes, because we really believe in forgiveness and new beginnings. To move from judgment to action we depend on the virtue of hope, the beckoning of an attractive future.

Conversely, if we want to maintain the gap between judgment and action we tend to denigrate the future and indulge our feelings of despair. If nothing is likely to change, or people are all no good, we can preserve our status as mere talkers. We don't have to put our judgments and selves on the line. Hopelessness greatly abets inaction. Do-nothings seldom love the future. Digging in their heels, delaying and overexamining, they would take the heart out of young people's enthusiasm and make mock of old people's suspicion that more is yet to be revealed.

In life-cycle terms, this is the misfiring of the developmental process. People who do not generate the fruitfulness demanded by their middle years cannot put together the integrity asked of them as they near the end; thus they tend to depreciate all vigorous doing. True, young people can despair of gaining an identity; suicide is high among adolescents. But the people who thwart the overall thrust of society into a better future almost always are the fairly aged, who tend to control the money and the politics.

Consider, for instance, the upper-management types who keep control mainly by inaction. Having somehow come to positions of great influence in their institutions, they have determined that the best way to defuse movements for changes they don't want is to let the paper pile up.

One such local manager regularly guts the enthusiasm of his subordinates by slowing all progress to a crawl. Pleading busyness, the need to consult with lawyers, the need to study all the ramifications, and a host of other plausible excuses, he waits until boredom or disillusionment has halved the opposition. Then with exquisite timing he announces the decision he intended from the beginning, his defense of the status quo. Mornings he tells the mirror that such delaying saves him from angry confrontations and keeps him sufficiently noncontroversial to function well in his important job. Evenings the people who suffer from his management philosophize that they would respect him a lot more, and feel much more attached to the institution, if he would say where he stands, explain his criteria, and let the chips fall where they would.

Even allowing for the insincerity that may mottle this last point of view when it comes to the actual political battling, the manager would do well to take it to heart. For were he to interrogate it honestly, the mirror would tell him (at least in indirect, glinting ways) that he is not really proud of his philosophy of inaction, that he finds it depressing and laden with guilt. He would feel much better, the mirror would suggest, if he took the proposals given him, studied them fully but speedily, and then met with the proposers to give them his appraisals. In such meetings he might find reasons to amend his appraisals or ways to strike a good compromise. But even if he had to give his subordinates a verdict of rejection, he could do it with a clean conscience: "I'm sorry that we differ in our assessments of the situation. You've made your analysis clear to me, and I hope I've made my disagreements with that analysis clear to you. Since I have the responsibility for the final decision, I must follow this negative judgment I have come to. I shall try to stay open to your reactions in the future. I hope that you will continue to presume my goodwill, accepting the fact that I have no choice but to do what I think best."

Such a speech probably would not spare the man all backbiting and gossip. Some detractors probably would continue to snipe at his reputation. But he would be able to say in all sincerity that such people are not worth paying much heed. Having satisfied himself that there was no cowardly gap between his judgment and his brave action, he could await each morrow expectantly.

Freedom

People who suffer no significant gaps between their judging and their doing are spiritually free. Freedom essentially is the capacity to do what we should, and we should above all enact the fruits of our best judgments. Conversely, bondage is the incapacity to do what we should. It shows in the gaps between our judgments and our actions. Because they do not follow through on their judgments, people in bondage don't get the correction and readjustment that free people do. All human learning is to a great extent a matter of trial and error. Few people can avoid the pattern of making their best judgments, acting upon them, and then reassessing those judgments in the light of what the action has revealed. Only those who do the truth come to the light, the Johannine theory has it (3:21). Those who will not act upon the best light they have hunker down in a deepening dishonesty.

To be sure, this is not the view of "freedom" that dominates the ads of the Sunday newspaper. There freedom is the ability to buy whatever catches one's eye, go wherever one's fancy would take one, paw all the pleasure one desires. The dissociation of all this from judgment, the bracketing of the whole so that it never touches responsibility, shows its bondage to the powers of darkness. If any of us were to subject the Sunday newspaper to the demanding test of the New Testament's view of human nature, we would emerge sobered by our culture's paganism. Much of such paganism is ignorance, of course, the work of superficial minds. But more of it is clever calculation, the manipulation of readers for big bucks.

Thus when people like Barbara conquer their addiction to television and sensationalist news, to think things over by the light of the moon, they start a journey that may only end deep in the counterculture of religion. The greatest enemy of modern advertising, modern economics, and modern politics is reflection. Action rooted in deep reflection, brave deeds expressing strong judgments about the truth, are positively unpatriotic—if patriotism means supporting the unreflective culture at large.

Not many of us are free enough to live a radically counter-culture lifestyle. Most of us choose to, or have to, make our bread and take our seat in the status quo. Most of us therefore are relatively enslaved, freer to buy stuff than think creatively, to love cars and clothes more than the grace of the Holy Spirit. To be sure, we are better off than people who lack life's necessities and people who lack civic freedom. But our very economic prosperity and apparent civic freedom can prove our spiritual undoing. Economic solvency and hedonistic mobility are not the core of spiritual freedom. Spiritual freedom comes from having no treasure but the mystery of God.

The mystery of God is the treasure that produced the giants human history most reveres. Moses, Zoroaster, Jeremiah, Plato, Confucius, Buddha, Lao-tzu, Jesus, Muhammad, and the other great seers all were counter-cultural. Confucius, for example, perhaps the hardest case to make, was not in his lifetime the orthodox figure that later Chinese centuries made him. He never gained the political office to which he aspired. He resolutely opposed the pragmatism that was making the China of his day a bloody battleground. The Way that he heard in the morning, the beauty that allowed him to die content at night, stressed inner goodness (*jen*) and outer social grace (*li*). The very suggestion of living for sensual pleasure, money, or crass political power the master would have found despicable.

When we are free, it follows, we honor the mystery at the center of human time. Building on the call to Israel recorded in Deuteronomy 6, Jesus made his first commandment the love of this mystery—with whole mind, heart, soul, and strength. People who obey Jesus immediately find themselves free of the seductions of the Sunday newspaper. Having thrust all tawdry or passing things back into their subordinate places, such people use creature comforts sparingly. Insofar as creature comforts fit in with a life pivoted on the mystery of God, they may be useful and gain our respect. Insofar as they want to take over the center of our lives, or refuse to be merely instruments of higher purposes, they merit our stern rejection.

Muhammad implied the same lesson when he taught that the greatest sin is idolatry. Those who do not keep free of things, are not wholly focused on the sole God, in effect are polytheists, people of divided religious allegiance. Many people in our Western churches need to hear this old Muslim teaching. Its translation into biblical terms is the familiar, "You cannot serve God and mammon."

When we are free of external glitter, not dominated by our passions or possessions, our peace and joy will take wing. If the mystery that makes everything be is for us, who can be against us? If we are realistic to the degree that we think frequently about our small place in the overall scheme of things, not many happenings will throw us off stride. In affluent countries such as the United States, a major tragedy is the self-chosen bondage of so many. Where they might be free to enjoy God's marvelous world, millions entrap themselves in baubles. Then the brave actions they contemplate seem to carry too high a price tag. To be a responsible, conscientious person might imperil that sports car, might force one to make do with nondesigner jeans.

When Barbara Took Charge

These themes about responsibility and action were not so clear to me when I was having my talks with Barbara. Although they are staples in the theology of freedom, it took some practical experience with concrete people trying to become free for me to realize their actual applications. Barbara herself was the best early example I found of a person steadily widening her range of self-knowledge, step by step walking into a greatly expanded liberty. As she gained confidence about her judgment, Barbara came closer and closer to making the hard decisions that eventually turned her life around. When it came time to act on the ground-level judgment that her old marriage was completely finished, and with it her naïveté, she was ready to take charge of a new phase of her journey.

Looking around her California setting, Barbara realized that much in it never had fit her. She had gone west with her husband, as a sort of adjutant prospector. The thrill of the chase after gold had kept him wide-eyed all the while they had lived together. For her, however, the thrill quickly had turned to panic. So the California scene, despite all she could find in it to praise (when she would step back from her own particular story), gave little allure to her future. She had family back East who supported her through the trials of the divorce, and when the dust settled she decided to go back to them and her roots. The support of her mother and brothers was the major attraction, since it loomed as a warm family circle for the boys. But the chance to make a new start on her own life was almost equally exciting. So, packing herself and the boys on a cross-country bus, she waved good-bye and hied herself back to New England. The little I know of her life since that departure day I've pieced together from a couple of letters and one visit.

The visit took place about a year after Barbara's departure, when I myself was back in New England. It was early fall, before the leaves had started to turn, but after the heat of the summer. I spent an afternoon at Barbara's mother's house, where she and the boys were still living. There had been plenty of room (Barbara's father had died soon after her marriage), and her mother was happy to have the house full again. The boys seemed much older, interested in things they never had mentioned in California. Barbara seemed a little shy and distant, but much more in control of her life. She had a job as a nurse in a local factory. She could arrange her hours rather flexibly and she found the work quite interesting. The boys seemed to have transplanted well, and they liked their new schools very much. The only problems lay in the area of socializing, and Barbara clearly was reluctant to discuss them with me. I realized that she wanted to end her old dependency, to call her time in California finished business.

So I left without probing how she hoped to handle the questions of new emotional involvements and a possible remarriage. Probably I should have told her that I sensed things like that no longer were my business, but I didn't sift out the visit until some time later, when the details finally fell into a pattern. Thus we parted rather awkwardly, with what I suspect was a mutual bit of sadness. Neither of us was wise enough to know how to move gracefully to a new form of friendship. I learned later that Barbara did remarry, but she never notified me herself. At the time I was hurt by her neglect. Now I think I understand the psychodynamics a little better, and I do not blame Barbara very much. Her shunting me to the fringes of her life probably was necessary if she was to gain a full liberation.

The "necessity" in such a move, of course, deserves some qualifications. In the best of worlds, with the best of maturations all around, we would always make changes gracefully. In the actual world, working with the limitations in ourselves and other people, many changes exact quite a toll. Thus it can seem the part of realism to cut oneself off from old patterns, memories, and even friends, in order to face the demands of a new situation with undivided energy. We see this negatively in the people who move into our area and spend their first six months telling us how much better things were back in their old locale. After a while we realize that they are simply trying to cope with the assaults of their new situation, telling tales of old victories because they are not sure how the new battles are going. But during their transition they can be rather gauche, and we wish they would put the past aside and join us in living in the present.

My considered interpretation of Barbara stresses the price she must have had to pay to adapt to her new situation. The return to her family likely had its trials, no matter how supportive their intentions. The move surely put special pressures on the boys, and so on their sympathetic mother. And Barbara's personal life as a very attractive single parent trying to decide about a second marriage must often have been taxing. For all their frequency, divorce and remarriage still carry many sanctions. In both the people trying to work out their implications, and the local cultures in which such people readjust, making a new life after a divorce seldom goes swimmingly.

Barbara did take charge and make herself a new life. She did survive and prosper. That should be enough for her counselor.

5.

Loving One's Life

The Outreach of Brave Action

People struggling with serious problems often become preoccupied with themselves and their problems, insulated from the rest of the world. At the outset it is natural that the counselee, the person in pain, will be the primary focus, but eventually this focus has to widen. The counselee can still remain the center, but the interconnections that tie that person to the rest of the world must at some point (not too far down the line) receive their due. The reality of any of our lives is that we live midst a web of reciprocal influences. What we eat, how we make our living, where we spend out money, how we vote, what our kids are experiencing at school all shape our selves, and so our joys and sorrows.

These connections emerge in any judgmental reflection that does its business. When we survey the influences on our insights, we at least nod in the direction of the whole ecology of creation. It is in acting out our judgments, however, that the realities of our ecological situation firmly impress themselves. Take the example of coming to the judgment that a friend is being mistreated at work and so deserves our active support. When we begin to pay out such support, writing letters or making contacts with other people who might help, we uncover some of the crisscrossings that interlace the work situation. To write a letter to our friend's boss involves estimating the boss's likely reaction. To determine the boss's likely reaction involves talking with some of the boss's friends or intimate colleagues. In such talks, we discover some of the constraints upon the boss's freedom.

Let's say, to make the example more concrete, that the problem concerns a temporary appointment that would be a good advancement for our friend. Assuming that she is well qualified for this temporary job and that the institution needs to improve its treatment of its female employees, we can start to probe the reasons why the appointment is not nearly automatic. What we likely will find is that "qualifications" are very flexible things, easily shuffled by the interested dealers and wheelers. Our friend may have a fine administrative record, but has she had any experience in sales? She may be smart as a whip, but does she make a sufficiently good impression?

Further, it usually turns out that our friend is not the only candidate for the new position. We may think that she clearly is the best candidate, but what do the "old boys" say? To their mind many of any woman's views are suspect of being faddish. "It is the traditional ways, tried and true, that have made this company's blue chip image. All the fuss one hears now about redeeming past sexual inequities is fine on the level of public relations, but woe to the company that lets it affect hard-core policy." "Amen, amen," the other woolly mammoths intone.

The person who has to make decisions in cases like our friend's must juggle many conflicting pressures.

The easiest course will be to maintain the present setting, just keep the old barge nosing along the line it has always hewn. So the most effective pressures will be those that combine some nod to this conservative instinct with solid arguments that our friend's appointment will benefit the whole corporation. By the time we've worked out these arguments, we've probably spent a week in heavy talking and late-night planning. We have met the enemy, and found it to be an octopus. The outreach of brave action is like casting a statue of a Hindu deity. We need four sets of eyes, to survey every direction, and three pairs of arms, to handle all the byplay to the sides.

Exhausting as this tends to be, it can make us realistic in ways the inactive never can be. Having entered the political arena, we find it is not just the sandpit where the dogs snarl and bite. It is also all the aisles by which the onlookers assemble, all the tunnels and back rooms where the dogs are housed and provisioned. Good politicians tap into information about every aspect of the arenas in which they fight. The substance of their work is giving and receiving information, gluing and ungluing deals. Few ordinary people have the talent or stamina for this work, but any ordinary person who wants to follow through on good judgments has to come to grips with the systematic quality of the political order. The flow charts in the city manager's office show only half the actual story. People not even listed on the charts can be the key to solving a given problem. Relations that ought to have no political significance (family ties, religious associations, old school friendships) can be the real channels of power.

Maybe this labyrinthine quality of politics explains why so few politicians are significant thinkers. Mastering the ever-changing flow of influence takes so much energy, and is so extroverted a work, that only the rarest politicians will have the capacity to digest their experience and make of it something profound. But this brings us back to the classical political dilemma, foreseen by Plato almost twenty-five hundred years ago. If we do not have wise people ("philosophers") running our public affairs, how can we avoid chaos? The obvious answer is that we cannot avoid it, and so are not a healthy, cooperative society. What does this mean for our counsel on how to make it through the day?

The Reality of Mystery

It means that we must confess we live in the midst of a mystery, a fullness or apparent complexity that we shall never comprehend. We may realize this ground-level fact through excursions into the political order or by tracing our own life history. If a person such as Barbara might have encountered the complexity of human affairs by trying to help a friend get a well-merited appointment, it was the tapestry of her own life history that in fact opened Barbara's eyes. She saw that the attitudes she had brought to her marriage had come from her parents and New England small-town culture. In California a different set of attitudes had dominated. The new factor of affluence made a big contribution. The women's movement, Eastern religions, humanistic psychology, computer technology, and other forces on the California scene played a role. Much as she might initially have considered her marital problems narrowly circumscribed, Barbara soon realized that she was not a solitary island. She was a personal place in a four-dimensional world, intersected in all directions.

The mind begins to feel overloaded when it

contemplates the complexity of such interactions, and to escape burning out it pivots into a new mode of operation. This new mode is as old as the Hindu Upanishads, where one can see ancient sages groping for a handle on life's multiplicity. Some of the most profound religion, Western as well as Eastern, comes from such groping after unity. In recent Christian terms, it forces us to deal with God's qualitative difference from the things of creation, God's strict mystery. The God capable of undergirding the multiplicity of our experience is not just another being, just another item (however grand) on the list. He-She-It is rather what one philosopher has called the Beginning and Beyond of the whole creational process.

There is a mystery at the beginning of any human life, yours, mine, or Barbara's. It is not removed by theories such as the Big Bang, which don't say why the creational process ever exploded. So the basic question, as philosophers from Leibniz to Heidegger have intuited, is why there is something rather than nothing. The traditional Christian answer is that for anything to exist something must exist independently, self-sufficiently. We call this something God. And to bring this something down from the realm of mere ideas and into the hurly-burly of our own too-solid flesh, we need only realize that *we* are beings begging explanation. The self-sufficient Being must be the explanation of us. Then God becomes the personal source suspected at the origin of our dance through space and time. We arrive on the scene and begin to move in our patterns because the architect of the cosmic processes decreed it. We could not be, or be as we are, without this creative decree.

Similarly, the Beyond of our lives and the world has about it the aura of mystery. If the process leading back to our beginning is too vast for human intelligence to comprehend (science but generalizes the few particulars it knows, and that quite hypothetically), so the term of the cosmic processes, the consummation point of the world, is a surplus of intelligibility no finite mind can factor. The way to deal with such mystery, whether we sense it as our Beginning or anticipate it as our Beyond, is to stop attacking it piecemeal and start appreciating it holistically. That is what our early morning and late night ruminations ought finally to produce: the holistic appreciation called contemplation. When we let our anxieties, plans, and questions finally fall away, we receive an "answer" from the mystery directly, as heart speaks to heart.

The answer is not a piece of information. It is not something we can diagram. Rather it is a reordering of our little being, an acceptance of finitude and ignorance. Letting go of our pretensions to mastering the world, we enter into a mode of unknowing. As spiritual classics such as the *Cloud of Unknowing* portray it, unknowing makes the mystery of God present, the limitlessness of God actual. Then we deal with Beginning/Beyond as far (transcendent) sides of our present existences. Then we pay more attention to the horizon of our consciousnesses, their contexts and foundations, than to their empirical data, or even their ideas and judgments. Slowly our "heart," the center of our whole selves, beats simply *toward* the darkness of God. As we come to love the divine mystery more intensely, our contemplation of it simplifies. We may still use images of Jesus or personal names like *Father.* But these are in the service of enjoying, or letting ourselves be purified by, the divine mystery itself.

In ages past, the divine mystery could be approached as though it dealt only with separate, individual souls. Today we can also approach it ecologically, as the mystery overshadowing (and linking) all of us myriad creatures. Beside the omnipresence of the divine mystery, the "omnirelevance" of the divine Beginning and Beyond, the complex systems of our politics and social interactions fade to the status of child's play. The mystery dominating the prayerful, contemplative consciousness is the force at work in the subatomic world and the world of the most distant stars. It is the force moving the sap of the plants, the blood of the animals, the neurons of human beings. In all this complexity it is the simplest reality, the elemental love-force making whatever is be. When we fall in love with it, we start loving the whole world.

Practical Wisdom

If there is one task that life sets us, one charge we must fulfill before we end our days, it is to love the whole world and labor for the whole world's prospering, despite the finitude, evil, and death afflicting each of the world's parts. Should we come to our end with such love, saying yes to all that (from the perspective of the finish) somehow "had" to be, we would be round successes. Should we not be able to muster such love, finish our time hateful or unsurrendering, our success would hang in brackets. Thus, the most practical wisdom any of us can grow, and the perennial reason for religion, is the strength to love life in the face of death, to respond "amen" to our history. Surprisingly enough, there are many prods to this ultimate wisdom, and many ways that it clarifies the task of making it through the day.

Among the many prods to this ultimate wisdom are sunrise, sunset, and the rain that falls on just and unjust alike. As most premodern peoples have known, nature is the great instructor in life's ultimate wisdoms. We are simply people, and our lives are short. None of us has ever seen God. Millions of years before us the everlasting hills were making quiet obeisance to the Creator. Millions of years after us distant stars will twinkle in praise. The great virtue of nature is that it is what it is, does what it should do, without a lot of self-conscious fuss. True, we prize our reflective consciousness; we realize that our spirits give us a special distinction. But we should be magnanimous enough to realize that God has made his natural vestiges little less than the angels, too. The otter and beaver larking in the water, the dignified silvery birch—they too are sacramental and tell us of grace. It does not matter that biology has no category called *grace*. We are doing theology here. For theology (the search to understand our ultimate commitments to mystery), each creature in the world is a cipher of God, a small crack in the Creator's code.

Perhaps that is why elderly people often come so to love their flowers and cats. It is not just that their children have fled the nest or that more strenuous occupations are unattractive. It is that simple live things like flowers and cats point to the holistic mystery. Approaching their dissolution into that mystery, older people instinctively linger over such pointers. The cats that T.S. Eliot drew from his fertile brow, and who later danced so winningly on Broadway, are but artful expansions of this notion. Bustopher Jones, Growltiger, Old Deuteronomy and the rest suggest a whole world that is not so much subhuman as waiting for human appreciation. The same for the forest world of the Pygmies, the coastal world of the American Salish Indians, the enchanted world of the aboriginal Australian outback. Big cats, trees, fishes, and purple sunsets have told tribal humanity for hundreds of thousands of years that the creative force is sacred.

Children, artists, and creative scientists are so many more prods to our love of the world, as are those few egregious self-spenders we call our generation's "saints." Children see the world freshly, unblinkered by convention. For them it is not yet routinized; it still can be wondrous. Artists track little wonders to their cosmic lair, throwing light on all of our everydayness. The blue paintings of Picasso, the patriotic music of Smetana, the novels of Saul Bellow and Patrick White make more of the ordinary than the rest of us can see, and so consecrate the ordinary. The scientists who work on nature's front lines, pushing back the frontiers of our understanding, find themselves intrigued by surpluses of intelligibility, the ten questions that arise when any biological, astrophysical, or molecular problem is answered. For them the world is not inert or to be taken for granted. For them the world retains the raw energy it got when God flung it forth from nothingness.

Nor do the saints read us a different lesson. Their lonely prayer and their work with the poor, the sick, the uneducated, and the oppressed intimate that the Creator is even more precious than the creation, and that the human images of the Creator are worth a life's generous spending. In dark nights and clouds of unknowing, the saints romance the ultimate mystery. At first to their surprise, and later to their wry acceptance, they find that the ultimate mystery has long been romancing them. Why would the Being intelligent enough to create our universe in fact actually create it? What good would accrue to such a Maker, what personal benefit? The only analogue we can defend, our only solid suspicion, is the impulse of love that everywhere is creative. Love begets, supports, diffuses itself for the good of others. It is restless to increase the total store of beauty; it peacefully awaits the understanding of those it benefits. The saints are the best hints of such a divine love-power, but all things beautiful and bright point in its direction.

Which means that all things beautiful and bright can help us make it through the day. All things working to repair what has been fractured and made ugly, to enlighten what still squats in the dark, urge us to place finitude, evil, and death in the bigger frame of the Creator's more powerful love. There would be no world to house finitude, evil, and death had the Creator not issued it. Those who think the evil outweighs the good have not done their elementary contemplations, not made the basic comparisons of nothingness and being, Satan and Christ. Having given us a universe, how can the Creator fail to provide us the wherewithal to love the universe as a whole?

Love as a Here and Now Center

But how does it feel to love the world as a whole, and how does this consummate the dynamics of experiencing, understanding, judging, and acting? It feels like a marriage to mystery. It consummates the dynamics of consciousness by giving them the horizon and shine they have always sought. The result is a growing confidence that the biblical heart of the matter is true. The closest analogue to God is love. People who love their neighbors and their world abide in God, and God in them. Love, then, becomes the daily touchstone, the main fruit by which to know the quality of the life one is growing.

Let us begin with the notion of "marrying" into the mystery. It is grounded in the fact that wherever we go (after we have sensed the significance of life's surplus of meaning) we find the mystery has preceded us. If we go to a national park, trying to beat the heat and rise above the smog, we find that the shimmer of the moon over the lake whispers about the mystery, the circling of the hawk at dawn intimates there is a center. If we go on so pedestrian a trip as up and down the aisles of the supermarket, it strikes us that this profusion of supplies, despite all the human labor it represents, mainly testifies to the largess of God. The new baby of the friend we visit hushes our voice to tender praise. The tired spirit of the granny we return to the nursing home paints the mystery slightly dark. There is no place where the mystery does not precede us. Neither the highest heavens nor the deepest earth are an escape. Unless we come to terms with the mystery, we feel unrealistic or imprisoned. When we come to terms with the mystery, we feel a pervasive sense of togetherness, as though the whole world were our affair.

This pervasive sense of togetherness is like the mutuality that develops in marriage. Now more intensely, now less, we have the feeling that *mine* and *thine* are inappropriate, *our* is the proper adjective. If God has chosen to be the Beginning and Beyond of every aspect of our lives, then every aspect of our lives is something we share with God. I suspect this is the implication of the self-disclosure of God recorded in Exodus 3:14. There Moses, having asked God for God's name, receives the enigmatic answer, "I am who I am."

The point seems to be that the mere name *God* is not much of an identifier. Only over time, through experience, in trust, will the mystery reveal who and what it is. Moreover, this revelation will depend on our capacity to appreciate it. Communication, even between God and us, is a two-way flow of traffic. God can only transmit effectively if we are good receivers. And the full sort of revelation or transmission that the biblical notion of covenant implies is much more than just mind to mind. It is heart to heart: a sharing of time on the model of a marriage.

This sense of sharing time consummates the dynamics of consciousness because the whole thrust of our awareness, from the beginnings of attentive experience to the term of brave action, is to engage us with what is real. If mystery is the primordial reality of our world, then marriage to mystery fulfills the process that began when we first lit up with wonder. The saints who experience a marital union with God unmistakably, as something that God brings about and they cannot avoid, are mystics in the strict sense of the term. The rest of us, who only sense the marital dimension of our advance into the mystery dimly, are mystics in an accommodated sense: people in love with the beautiful whole but not yet dominated by it.

Still, even we can become increasingly convinced that the love of the mystery is our crux. Once we have tasted this surrendering love of the whole, no lesser horizon satisfies. Similarly, once the mystery has become our context for understanding any trouble or pleasure, no other context seems realistic. For example, the person dealing with sickness now finds that only by framing it as a gift of God does it reveal its full set of possibilities. Strange to say, even so threatening and painful an experience as sickness can bear us another revelation of the mystery. This does not mean that we should not struggle mightily to get well. It does not imply that God wants our sickness rather than our health. It just says that as long as we are suffering ill health we might as well try to see our trial as something that God would have us turn to profit. Be it a chance to realize our frailty, or the passingness of human vanities, or the temptations to despair that all the world's billions of sufferers face, our time of sickness can turn out to be a blessing, can instruct us more deeply in the ''otherness'' of God's ways.

Isaiah saw that God's ways are as distant from our instinctive human ways as the heavens are distant from the earth. Jesus knew that God's ways can bring a bitter cup we do not at all want to taste. Our marriage to mystery is too real for it not to force us to grow. The love of God is too deep for it not to have to transform us.

When Barbara came to see how connecting her life to the mystery might redeem her broken marriage, she gained considerable religious maturity. Having a real God would mean that nothing in her past, present, or future could not be turned to good account. A God she could live with and could come to know more deeply over time would mean that she could pick herself up and start moving again. It could even mean that one day she might feel she was better off for having suffered such a painful experience.

Barbara's Love of Life

On the basis of what I learned of her during our months of counseling, I have a good picture of how Barbara was developing a rich love of life. As I noted, my information about her development after her move back East is only sketchy, but by extending the lines of the growth I myself saw and adding the few details I learned about her life after her departure, I can sketch a portrait that seems to me highly probable. In rendering it here, I hope to suggest the modest fulfillment possible for almost all of us, if we come to appreciate God's mystery.

Four major concerns dominated Barbara's life at the end of my time with her. The first was her children. She took her responsibilities as a mother very seriously, but not because she thought of them as charges laid upon her. Her boys were her chief delight, and she loved them as naturally as she breathed. Without denying that they sometimes wore her out or that they were suffering from the divorce or even that she lavished upon them some of the love she used to give her husband, she regularly would say that they were the light of her life, an unending source of gladness. Even their differences fascinated her. The older boy was serious and self-contained, a fanatic about sports. The younger boy was playful, outgoing, and showed signs of being very bright. There was not much competition between them. The younger one clearly would outweigh the older by fifty pounds one day. And every bit of their contrast, interaction, and likely future relationship fascinated their mother. The signs of growth they manifested each day made each day a wonderful time. The cuts and bruises they suffered brought out the full nurse.

Nursing was Barbara's second major concern, and when she returned to it (after a break for the early years of child-rearing) she came to live it as a rewarding profession. In her student days it had been something to do while she waited to get married. She liked working with people and found satisfaction in easing pain, so it satisfied her emotionally. The science and bureaucracy were trials she was willing to bear. When she returned as a mature woman, however, she found much more potential for professional development. There was the possibility of specializing in areas such as surgery or intensive care. There were the possibilities of teaching and higher administration. So Barbara enrolled in a master's program and kept open the option of a doctorate. She took her studies seriously and did private work on the history and philosophy of nursing. Since nursing obviously suited her, she decided to use it as a modality for her personal growth. Why not enlarge her cultural horizons by looking at various phenomena, past and present, through the lens of nursing: healing sickness, nurturing health? Why not investigate economics, politics, and religion through their influences on health care? By the time Barbara had gotten up a head of steam about nursing and gained strong enthusiasm for her work, she found herself charged with energy. She was not at all inclined to mope at home about her problems.

The third focus in Barbara's expanding capacity for love was a marital relationship, and this of course was painful. The more she came to accept herself and view the worlds of her children and work positively, the more frustrating became her single status. Wounds lingered from the past. She rankled from mistreatments in the present, such as being invited out on a date and driven directly to a motel. But the hope of revealing her growing self to another person, of sharing life so as to divide its hurts and double its joys, kept her intensely interested in marriage. I was not surprised, therefore, to learn that she had remarried. I suspect she came to that step deliberately, taking a lot of time; but it seemed to me inevitable that many men would find her attractive, and likely that a few would be solid marital prospects.

The fourth focus, to which we gave special attention during our sessions, was the love of God through prayer. This was new to Barbara, and getting started on it took some doing. Previously she had thought of prayer only in terms of the vocal prayers she had learned in childhood. As the sense of a real, mysterious God emerged and began to connect up with depths of her quiet times of reflection, she began to hunger to pray with her own words, and then with no words at all. The two letters I received both emphasized the consolation such prayer was bringing her. She was very faithful to her morning and night sessions, because she found them as nourishing as breakfast and dinner. Barbara also went out of her way during my visit to repeat her commitment to prayer. It settled her down, she said, and made the hard times bearable.

So, when last glimpsed, Barbara's love of life was burning brightly at several points around the circle. If she has continued to grow and followed the predictable pattern, the fires at each point have moved toward one another, coming closer and closer to warming all of her life with a quiet religious love. Religious (mysterious) love has this tendency. The saints are able to find God (lovableness) in all things. No longer do they make much distinction between work and prayer, children and spouses. One warmth moves them through all the parts of their days. Thus they come to love life more and more holistically, the way the Spirit of God must love it.

Conclusion:
Kansas Living

A Regular Regime

From California to Connecticut or Kansas, people who want to cope better with the challenges of their days would do well to consider adopting a regular regime. By this I mean nothing rigid or inflexible, just a general form for channeling one's energies, trying to attain one's goals. Many people I've worked with have found that their lives improve significantly once they've worked out a regular regime. At least three factors seem to demand attention: meeting major responsibilities, providing for idiosyncratic needs, and ensuring that the build of one's days serves a deepening penetration of objective reality.

Most people's days are dominated by trying to meet their major responsibilities at work and to their families. In the past most of the work responsibilities fell upon men, and most of the family responsibilities fell upon women, but nowadays a majority of both sexes have to deal with both sets of responsibilities. Obviously, therefore, a regime—a way of structuring their time—that did not provide for what they have to do on the job and as parents and spouses would do most people little good. On the other hand, the harum-scarum way that a great many people approach both their work and their family does untold amounts of harm.

A good example of this might be the chaos wreaked by the wife of a friend of mine when she suddenly (unreflectively) changed jobs. She had been teaching at the same school as her husband, but she decided (for the lure of more money and better colleagueship) to take a similar job at another institution thirty miles away. What she did not consider were the changes her commuting this distance would bring, both to her own psyche and to the routine of her family. The family had only one car, so the husband had to rearrange all his transportation. The two institutions had different calendars, so the couple never found themselves with the same time off. The woman's new responsibilities at work began at 7:30 A.M. so early time with the children had to go. She now had staff meetings late in the afternoon, so the family's evening routine was disrupted. It was a mess, and one year of it brought the woman to her knees, begging to get her old job back.

What the couple discovered is that a family routine is both necessary and not completely flexible. Meals and bedtimes have to occur within relatively narrow limits. Time for spouses to be together does not occur automatically. Any regular regime worth its salt will set clear and reasonable times for such basics.

Second, any good regime also will allow individuals enough time to satisfy their idiosyncratic needs: listening to music, reading good books, getting hard exercise, trimming up the garden, making love when one is peaceful, making love when the other is not exhausted. Obviously a large household demands some compromises between what different individuals need and what the family must do together. But any workable regime will let individuals do the things that make them happiest, that enable them to function at their best. Any regime that does not is doomed to resentment and then failure.

The third key aspect is the regime's objectivity. Unless it arranges times and duties so that they serve the family's real growth, it is sound and fury signifying nothing. All that we have said about the build of consciousness—the need to increase attention, sharpen intelligence, deepen reflection, encourage action, and ignite outreaching love—comes home to roost quite practically. At work and play, prayer and socializing, only one thing finally is necessary: moving ahead into the mystery of God, becoming more obedient to Jesus' twofold commandment. Thus the realistic family's regime both takes its members into rich experiences and provides sufficient time for them to reflect and enact the implications of such experiences.

To make these considerations as concrete as possible, let me sketch one weekday routine that might enable many people to deal well with the three basic factors: 6:00 rise, 6:30 morning prayer/reflection, 7:00 breakfast, 8:00 work, 12:00 exercise/lunch, 1:00 work, 6:00 dinner/family time, 8:00 reading, 10:00 evening prayer/reflection, 10:30 retire. This is just a framework. All sorts of errands, entertainments, charitable helps, and special tasks would alter it day by day. But it might suit many people most workdays: about seven hours sleep (nap if more needed), a solid workday, exercise, prayer/reflection, family time, ongoing education. Big chores and special entertainment would mainly occur on weekends. Nights would be flexible—open to walks, talks, chores, friends.

With some such regular order, rhythm and regularity would pace a family through its days. A clear, disciplined option for productive work, prayer, culture, and deep sharing would defend it against trivialization by too much television or dissipation by mindless fun, unnecessary work, or useless gossip. Without becoming programmed like computers, family members could give themselves the chance to become more attentive to the world, more disciplined in probing their lives' meaning, more judicious about their biases, more generous in doing good, and more mystically attuned to Dante's "love that moves the stars." The quiet times of morning and evening would promote reflection and prayer. The driven times of midday would go into solid, socially useful work (schooling, in the case of children). Meals would be regular, as would exercise. Dinner would be a family affair, with few leaves granted. Culture and social service would rate at least as high as fun.

Making It through the Day

The phrase "making it through the day" clearly is just a motto for good—responsible, satisfying—living. If at first it has echoes of bare survival, in time it can swell to a splendid leitmotiv. Then we glimpse the glory that the churchman Irenaeus envisioned long ago: human beings fully alive. In my interpretation, both survival and glorious flourishing depend on an ongoing self-transcendence. When we are growing more intimate with the mysterious reality that is the bedrock of our lives, we are prospering. When we are fleeing this reality, or ignoring it, or failing to attune ourselves to its measure, we are failing. Other criteria of "success," such as our bank accounts or social status, shrink to insignificance. A mystical pauper is much richer than a dissolute millionaire.

The "day" through which we are all trying to

make it breaks down most basically into Freud's two great needs: love and work. For our waking hours, these are the giant challenges. Work is the fundamental way we love our neighbors and try to move the world forward. Love shows most clearly in our prayer, family life, and leisurely play. If we are working well, at significant tasks, we are stroking forward into generativity, the great psychological need of our mature years. If we are loving well, we are consolidating the identities we first congealed in adolescence, making steady progress toward the final amen that our deathbeds will require.

Work, of course, can demand and nourish great love. Without great love we will not serve the difficult tribal members graciously, nor long be very creative. Conversely, love demands hard work, for both its own development and the outreach of its goodwill. Regimes therefore have an easy way to check their objective efficacy: Are they nourishing good work and love? Self-transcendence, the maturation of our consciousnesses, also can be evaluated in these terms: Are we becoming better workers and lovers? So, by the ultimate standards we should most want to honor, we are making it if we are becoming more creative and useful at work, warmer and more patient in love. The creativity of work dovetails with a deep honesty. The service of work connects with deep senses of justice and compassion.

Let the wife of my friend also illustrate these truisms. Back at her old job, chastened and wiser, she began to rethink her work in less selfish, more objective terms. Whereas previously it had been the source of her paycheck and haughty self-image, in review it showed potential for ''poetry'' (creative making) and service. Thus the woman began to hone her lectures, shaping them more artistically. She unbent with her students, offering them a motherly care. She found a solid piece of research, with large social implications. At home she also changed things for the better. Having missed regular time with her kids, she started reintroducing herself to them. Realizing her husband had gotten lost in her shuffle, she apologized and started thinking up good things for them to share. And for herself she provided regular time for music, her favorite contemplative outlet. To her surprise, this disciplining of her time did not make her more compulsive but freer. Knowing how most of her days would unfold, she had fewer anxieties. In her bones she knew that both her love and her work were flourishing, and this filled her with a humble satisfaction.

Such humble satisfaction makes the struggles of ordinary living worthwhile. More, it tells us we are greatly blessed. Because we are doing the main things we have to do and feeding our main hungers, we feel that most is right with our world. Ordered within, we can resist, and somewhat heal, the disorders raging without. Were the rest of the world to discipline itself and come to feel blessed, happy to be here, a majority of its fits and spasms would cease. People treat one another like wolves because they do not know the things for their peace. Because they are wolfish, however, they tempt their leaders (who themselves know little about inner order and peace) to oppressive laws and economic regimes. That is the basic plot line of modern politics: people with little wisdom prescribing and executing regimes that oppress the human spirit.

Those with political talents can use their sense of blessedness as a base from which to oppose such regimes. Having a strong sense of what makes for peace and joy, they can say yea or nay most cogently. Ordinary citizens, like Barbara and most of us, will witness indirectly by the contrary drift of our lives. Above all, our reflection and prayer will hold a mirror to the disorders of modernity. (Not that medieval or ancient times were simon-pure; just that modernity has sold contemplation to technology.) If we center ourselves outside profit and pleasure, we will both instruct our irreligious neighbors and affront them. That will make for interesting subplots and byplays.

Our job is to be peaceful and joyous because we are growing wiser by the year. If we do our job, people with eyes to see and ears to hear will recognize a good example. The others will have to depend on God's mercy, which we will know from experience is great.

Appendix:
The Method
Summarized

1. *Pay attention:* Sharpen your awareness of what is going on around you. Even more, sharpen your awareness of what is going on inside you, your feelings of joy and sadness.

2. *Be intelligent:* Discipline yourself to probe your experience with a keen will to understand. Draw diagrams, play games, push the data back and forth. Dispose yourself so that (most likely in a time of relaxation) you will get a flash of insight, generate a bright idea, that will organize your experience more meaningfully.

3. *Be judicious:* Reflect on your bright ideas. Check on the way you gained them. Look for biases in yourself that may have slanted your perception or interpretation of the data. Recognize your deep hunger to throw off what is illusory, to engage with what is real.

4. *Act bravely:* Follow through on the practical implications of your good judgments. Stop being just a thinker or a talker and become a doer. Suffer the trial and error process of testing your judgments in the hard world of work and politics. Bandage your cuts

and bruises gently and humorously. Refuse to be divided, alienated, a coward condemned by your own conscience.

5. *Love mysteriously:* Let your affection for the real world disclosed by your judgments and brave actions flower. Ponder the primordial question: Why is there something rather than nothing? Appreciate the surplus of meaning and beauty at every turn. Make the crucial comparison between being and nonbeing, goodness and evil, Jesus and Satan. Pray to the mysterious fullness of being, your Creative Source, more and more simply. Let the holistic love of this prayer become the hallmark of your life. Note how much better you are making it through the day.

John Carmody is Adjunct Professor of Religion at Wichita State University, Wichita, Kansas. He received his Ph.D. degree from Stanford University in California.

Dr. Carmody has written many books, including *Theology for the 1980s, Religion: The Great Questions,* and *Becoming One Flesh,* which he coauthored with his wife, Dr. Denise Lardner Carmody.

The Carmodys enjoy jogging and classical music.